Seasons of Waiting

"The Bible and the history of the church are full of stories of God revealing incredible dreams and rescuing men and women in dramatic settings, such as Moses, Mary, John Wesley, and Pascal. But of course, it does not always happen that way—as Hannah, Elizabeth, Jeremiah, and countless other believers through the ages can testify. In *Seasons of Waiting*, Betsy Childs Howard offers hope for the weary traveler wrestling with this tension. Through her own story and those of others, she demonstrates how to wait well upon the faithful One who knows us and loves us and has a plan and purpose for each of us—and who often surprises us with gifts of which we may have never dreamed."

Ravi Zacharias, Founder and President, Ravi Zacharias International Ministries; author, *Jesus Among Other Gods*

"The thesis of this book is simple but profound: God does not leave us alone in the many 'waiting rooms' of life, but uses seasons of pain, absence, and longing to draw us unto himself. Deeply personal and biblically wise, this is a book every Christian should read."

Timothy George, Founding Dean, Beeson Divinity School; General Editor, Reformation Commentary on Scripture

"We are all in a season of waiting, even in the moments when we think we have arrived. Betsy Childs Howard speaks comforting truth to our anxious hearts, especially when we worry that our waiting will never end. What are you waiting for? Get a copy of this book and ask a friend to read with you!"

Gloria Furman, pastor's wife, Redeemer Church of Dubai; author, *The Pastor's Wife* and *Missional Motherhood*

"Betsy leads us with a gentle strength through some of the most difficult seasons of waiting and points us to Christ. This book will be a great encouragement to many. I hope you read it and draw near to your Savior who sees, loves, and cares about you in every situation."

Jessica Thompson, author, *Everyday Grace*; coauthor, *Give Them Grace*

"No matter who you are, you're waiting for something. Indeed, Christianity is a waiting religion as we eagerly long for the return of Christ. I don't know a better book on the topic than this one by Betsy Childs Howard, one of my favorite writers."

Collin Hansen, Editorial Director, The Gospel Coalition; author, *Blind Spots*

"Waiting is hard and confusing; and oftentimes our longings are for good things, like marriage and children. Betsy Childs Howard has provided an excellent resource to help us wait well. She doesn't throw out familiar advice like 'guard your heart' and 'be content.' Instead, she graciously shows us how God is working in our waiting through the parables of Jesus, the stories of others, and the wonderful promises in God's Word. God has a purpose greater than we could ever hope or imagine and Howard gently takes our hand to help us see this to be true. You will not regret picking this up."

Trillia Newbell, author, *Enjoy, Fear and Faith,* and *United*

Seasons of Waiting

Walking by Faith When Dreams Are Delayed

Betsy Childs Howard

WHEATON, ILLINOIS

Seasons of Waiting: Walking by Faith When Dreams Are Delayed

Copyright © 2016 by Betsy Childs Howard

Published by Crossway
    1300 Crescent Street
    Wheaton, Illinois 60187

Cover design: Connie Gabbert

First printing 2016

Printed in the United States of America

Unless otherwise indicated, Scripture quotations are from the ESV® Bible (The Holy Bible, English Standard Version®), copyright © 2001 by Crossway, a publishing ministry of Good News Publishers. Used by permission. All rights reserved.

Scripture quotations marked NASB are from *The New American Standard Bible®*. Copyright © The Lockman Foundation 1960, 1962, 1963, 1968, 1971, 1972, 1973, 1975, 1977, 1995. Used by Permission.

Scripture references marked NIV are taken from The Holy Bible, New International Version®, NIV®. Copyright © 1973, 1978, 1984, 2011 by Biblica, Inc.™ Used by permission. All rights reserved worldwide.

All emphases in Scripture quotations have been added by the author.

Trade paperback ISBN: 978-1-4335-4949-6
ePub ISBN: 978-1-4335-4952-6
PDF ISBN: 978-1-4335-4950-2
Mobipocket ISBN: 978-1-4335-4951-9

Library of Congress Cataloging-in-Publication Data

Names: Howard, Betsy Childs, 1981–
Title: Seasons of waiting : walking by faith when dreams are delayed / Betsy Childs Howard.
Description: Wheaton : Crossway, 2016. | Includes bibliographical references and index. | Description based on print version record and CIP data provided by publisher; resource not viewed.
Identifiers: LCCN 2015045056 (print) | LCCN 2015037140 (ebook) | ISBN 9781433549502 (pdf) | ISBN 9781433549519 (mobi) | ISBN 9781433549526 (epub) | ISBN 9781433549496 (tp)
Subjects: LCSH: Expectation (Psychology)—Religious aspects—Christianity. | Trust in God—Christianity. | Waiting (Philosophy) | Patience—Religious aspects—Christianity.
Classification: LCC BV4647.E93 (print) | LCC BV4647.E93 H69 2016 (ebook) | DDC 248.4—dc23
LC record available at http://lccn.loc.gov/2015045056

Crossway is a publishing ministry of Good News Publishers.

RRD		26	25	24	23	22	21	20	19	18	17	16
15	14	13	12	11	10	9	8	7	6	5	4	3	2

To B.N.,
who was worth waiting for and is a joy to wait with
as together we long for Christ's appearing

Contents

Preface

What does your heart long for?

If you've picked up this book, there's a good chance you didn't have any difficulty answering that question. Most women are waiting for something, but some women are waiting acutely. The thing missing from their lives is in such sharp focus that they aren't sure they'll ever feel complete without it.

If that describes you, you know the truth of the proverb, "Hope deferred makes the heart sick" (Prov. 13:12). It's much easier to stop hoping than it is to have your dream deferred again and again. Of course, those who have been born again in Christ have the sure and certain hope of fullness of joy in God's eternal presence, but we aren't there yet. What do we do in the meantime?

This book is meant to help you answer that question. I hope you will read all the chapters, not just the one or two that apply to what you are waiting for the most. I firmly believe that to flourish in our many seasons of waiting, we need support from women in other stages of life who have different struggles and different strengths. I encourage you to seek out other women who are waiting, to find mutual encouragement and help each other to wait well.

This book talks about "seasons" of waiting, but I fully recognize that your waiting season may not end in this life. Even if that is the case, if you are a believer in Jesus, your waiting will still only last for a season, because this life on earth is only the anteroom of your life to come. It is right that we should long for that day. I hope this book will stir in you a desire to wait with eagerness for the return of Jesus and the fullness of God's kingdom.

1

The School of Waiting

To those who have seen
The Child, however dimly, however incredulously,
The Time Being is, in a sense, the most trying time of all.

W. H. Auden, "For the Time Being"

Betty's husband, a teacher in his early sixties, just lost his job. They aren't financially ready for retirement, but few schools want to hire a teacher who is over sixty. They are praying for God to provide a new job, but they don't know when or where that might be.

Grace and her husband are both eager for a baby. It is taking longer than she would like. She has a history of thyroid problems, and it's possible that this will affect her ability to conceive. She doesn't know whether her longing for a baby will stretch on for years or whether her next pregnancy test will be positive.

Catherine has cerebral palsy. She's been relatively independent for most of her life, but now she is wheelchair bound and has recurring problems with a wound on her foot that will not heal. She spends her time going to different doctors, none of whom have been able to cure her painful, debilitating wound.

These women are all friends of mine.[1] Their life situations are very different, but they are each waiting on God for something. None of them knows how long their waiting will last or why God is asking them to wait. They are students in the school of waiting.

. . . .

When I was in school, I was a conscientious student. I tried hard to do my best and learn my lessons because students who learn please their teachers and advance to new assignments.

When it comes to my life, there's a part of me that wants to please God in the same way I tried to please my teachers. When a trial comes my way, I assume that God has sent it and that he wants me to learn something from it before moving on to the next assignment. This kind of thinking helps me trudge forward in the hope that the trial will end shortly if I play the role of attentive student. But this kind of thinking does not serve me well when God takes me into the school of waiting.

You see, for God, the goal of this school is not that I should learn my lesson so that I don't have to wait anymore. God wants me to learn how to wait so that I can *wait well*, even if my waiting continues for the rest of my life. While my plan is to keep a chipper attitude and show God that I'm a good student so he will bring my waiting to a close, God wants something even better for me. Rather than end my waiting, he wants to bless my waiting.

In his book *Waiting on God*, Andrew Murray explains God's gentle instruction:

At our first entrance into the school of waiting upon God, the heart is mainly set on the blessings which we wait for. God graciously uses our needs and desires for help to educate us for something higher than we were thinking of. We were seeking gifts; He, the Giver, longs to give Himself and to satisfy the soul with His goodness. It is just for this reason that He often withholds the gifts, and that the time of waiting is made so long. He is constantly seeking to win the heart of His child for Himself. He wishes that we would not only say, when He bestows the gift, "How good is God!" but that long before it comes, and even if it never comes, we should all the time be experiencing: it is good that a man should quietly wait. "The LORD is good unto them that wait for him."

What a blessed life the life of waiting then becomes, the continual worship of faith, adoring, and trusting His goodness. As the soul learns its secret, every act or exercise of waiting becomes just a quiet entering into the goodness of God, to let it do its blessed work and satisfy our every need.[2]

God is working in our waiting.

You may have picked up this book in the hope that it will help you learn your lesson (and thereby bring your waiting to an end). My hope is that it will help you learn to love waiting, to want to wait well, and to see that God has a beautiful kingdom purpose that he is bringing about through (not in spite of) your waiting.

The Purpose You Already Know About

I doubt that the idea that waiting on God can be purposeful is a new one to you. If you are familiar with the doctrine of sanctification, you know that God can use any experience to make you more and more like himself. For example, in the book of

James, we are commanded to count trials as joy, knowing that the testing of faith produces steadfastness (James 1:2–3). Waiting can certainly be a test of faith, and these verses promise that waiting can produce a steadfast character.

Likewise, the letter to the Hebrews talks about the sanctifying work of God's discipline. It says that discipline leads to holiness, and that it will produce "the peaceful fruit of righteousness" (Heb. 12:9–11). Waiting is part of discipline, isn't it? The discipline of a little child involves teaching him to wait his turn or to wait for dessert. It is not good for a child to get everything he wants. In the same way, God's discipline through waiting is good for us and will lead to deeper peace and good fruit in our lives.

Waiting exposes our idols and throws a wrench into our coping mechanisms. It brings us to the end of what we can control and forces us to cry out to God. God doesn't waste our waiting. He uses it to conform us to the image of his Son.

But sanctification is not the only purpose God has in mind when he takes us into the school of waiting. When we wait, God gives us the opportunity to live out a story that portrays the gospel and serves as a kingdom parable.

Every Story Whispers His Name

Families around the world have grown to love *The Jesus Storybook Bible*, a children's Bible by Sally Lloyd-Jones. I confess that, though I don't have children, I have my own copy and have benefited greatly from it. In *The Jesus Storybook Bible*, Sally Lloyd-Jones writes:

> There are lots of stories in the Bible, but all the stories are telling one Big Story. The Story of how God loves his children and comes to rescue them.

It takes the whole Bible to tell this Story. And at the center of the Story, there is a baby. Every Story in the Bible whispers his name. He is like the missing piece in a puzzle— the piece that makes all the other pieces fit together, and suddenly you can see a beautiful picture.[3]

One story at a time, Lloyd-Jones shows how each of the stories found in the Old Testament points in some way to Jesus. Not only does the ram in the thicket provided for Abraham point to the Lamb of God, the Tower of Babel and the healing of Namaan point to Christ as well!

One reason I love *The Jesus Storybook Bible* is that it depicts the Old Testament's future-oriented thrust. Old Testament stories do not stand alone, rather they unfurl like a red carpet rolled out to welcome a king. Jesus is the sacrifice pictured at Passover, the deliverer foreshadowed by Moses, and the King prefigured by David.

Waiting figures prominently in many of the stories of the Old Testament. Moses waited for Pharaoh to let God's people go. Joseph waited in a prison cell. Hannah waited for a baby. These stories are true stories, but they are also small-scale versions of the bigger story: Israel was waiting on God to fulfill his promises.

God fulfilled his promises to send a deliverer, the Messiah, by sending his Son, Jesus. Even so, God did not stop using stories of waiting to tell his story because the waiting isn't over yet. Jesus died and rose again, and then he ascended to sit at the right hand of God where he is to this day. The New Testament portrays the ascended Jesus as the Bridegroom who has gone away but will return (Matt. 25:1–13; Mark 2:20). Our waiting is different this side of the cross. We know now whom we are waiting for, but the waiting isn't easy. There should be a future thrust to our faith, just as there was a future thrust in the stories that make up the Old Testament.

We are still waiting in the same ways that our favorite Bible characters waited. Some of us are waiting for a bridegroom. Some of us are waiting for a baby. Some are waiting for a home. Some are waiting for a prodigal child or a prodigal spouse. Some await healing and an end to pain. Above all, we are all waiting for the return of Jesus.

Until the Messiah came, Scripture's stories of waiting reminded old covenant believers that all was not right with the world. Marriage covenants were broken. Wombs were empty. Israel needed reconciliation with God.

In the same way, our waiting should remind us and all new covenant believers that *all is not right with the world*. While Jesus has died and risen, he has not yet come again. Paul describes the second coming of Christ this way: "Then comes the end, when he delivers the kingdom to God the Father after destroying every rule and every authority and power. For he must reign until he has put all his enemies under his feet" (1 Cor. 15:24–25). We are still waiting for that victory.

Shouldn't I Be Content?

If your waiting is characterized by painful longing, you may feel guilty about that. We are supposed to be content with the life God has given us, right? If I am consumed by desire for something he hasn't given me, that must be sinful discontentment, mustn't it?

Yes and no. Yes, our waiting should be undergirded with a firm confidence in the goodness of God. We should believe steadfastly that God is our loving Father who only gives us what is good (Matt. 7:7–11). We can know with certainty that his "divine power has granted to us all things that pertain to life and godliness" (2 Pet. 1:3). Like the apostle Paul, our contentment must be based in the sufficiency of Christ, not in satisfactory temporary circumstances (Phil. 4:10–13).

In spite of these truths, a persistent longing does not mean that you are indulging in sinful discontentment. The same Paul who wrote that he had learned to be content in every circumstance wrote that he had "great sorrow and unceasing anguish" (Rom. 9:2) when he considered his fellow Jews who had rejected the gospel. Waiting well doesn't mean waiting without pain.

What if Hannah had resigned herself to childlessness instead of pouring out her prayers to God with her tears? What if the father of the Prodigal Son had dried his eyes and moved on, rather than watching and waiting for his wayward one to come home? What if Hosea, instead of grieving over his wife's unfaithfulness, had proclaimed that this was God's will and he was probably better off without her?

If these biblical characters had suppressed their pain and put on a happy face, we would be missing the deep bass notes that give the gospel such sweet resonance. If there are no tears, then the promise that God "will wipe away every tear from their eyes" (Rev. 21:4) would not be necessary.

Your Waiting Is a Parable

In this book, I will talk about five life situations that involve painful waiting. I've chosen these five areas because they are prominent biblical themes, but they are also scenarios that are still common to God's people. If you are waiting for a spouse that has yet to appear, for a pregnancy that you haven't been able to conceive or carry, for healing that may or may not come, for a home that you never have to leave, or for a prodigal child or spouse to return, you are living a parable. A parable is a story with a point. The story of your waiting can portray—to you and to others—God's salvation history, both up to this point and still to come.

If that sounds strange to you, consider some other life scenarios that are commonly recognized as depictions of the gospel. How many weddings have you been to at which the minister told the couple that their marriage represents Christ and the church? This idea comes straight from the Bible itself, specifically Ephesians 5:22–23. Paul tells the Ephesians that the love a husband shows his wife—a love that places her needs above his own—represents the love that Christ has for the church. Conversely, a wife who submits to her husband portrays the church's trusting submission to the headship of Christ.

Or take adoption. In Romans 8:14–17, Paul explains that those who believe in Jesus have been adopted by his Father into the family of God. We've been given the right to call on him, and he has made us his heirs. Adoption gives a child all of the rights and privileges of one who is born into a family. Adoptive parents powerfully portray the love of God by choosing to make their own that which was once not their own. They are a parable of our God who took a people (Israel) and made them his own and who takes people (us) and makes them his beloved children.

Throughout the Scriptures, God uses different analogies and word pictures that portray waiting on the Lord. In the book of James, he compares waiting for the Lord's return to waiting for a harvest:

Be patient, therefore, brothers, until the coming of the Lord. See how the farmer waits for the precious fruit of the earth, being patient about it, until it receives the early and the late rains. You also, be patient. Establish your hearts, for the coming of the Lord is at hand. (James 5:7–8)

Every time a farmer sows his field, weeds his garden, or waters a crop that is not yet bearing fruit, he is a living picture of how we should wait on the return of the Lord. We must be patient, and we must hope in what we do not yet see.

Farmers generally have an idea of how long it will take their crops to grow. Late rains may delay a crop by weeks, but not by months or years. I have to think that patience is a bit easier when you have some idea of how long the waiting might last. In the seasons covered in this book, we don't ordinarily know how long we will be waiting. That's what makes waiting so hard! It may last for a lifetime. But in that sense, our waiting is an even better parable of what it means to wait for the coming of the Lord. Christ could come tomorrow, or he may not return in our lifetime. A key component of Christian waiting is learning how to keep watch without becoming impatient or cynical.

Parables Can Be Missed

People commonly think that Jesus told parables to make the truth easier to understand. But the Bible presents parables as stories with meanings that can be easily missed. When Jesus's disciples asked him why he taught in parables, he made it clear that they weren't simply illustrations:

And he answered them, "To you it has been given to know the secrets of the kingdom of heaven, but to them it has not been given. For to the one who has, more will be given, and he will have an abundance, but from the one who has not, even what he has will be taken away. This is why I speak to them in parables, because seeing they do not see, and

21

hearing they do not hear, nor do they understand." (Matt. 13:11–13)

You see, parables reveal, but they can also conceal. Those with hearts awakened by the Spirit have eyes to see the kingdom of heaven; they know how to look at an earthly analogy and see the heavenly meaning beyond it. Those with hard hearts can't see past the analogy. They hear the story but miss the point. They are like babies who stare at a pointing finger instead of at what is being pointed out.

Parables are signs that can be heeded or missed completely. The kingdom of God is hidden unless you have eyes to see it. For those who don't have ears to hear, both the good news and the hard truths of a parable go in one ear and out the other.

God has given you a parable. Each different kind of waiting shines light on a different facet of the gospel story. Only those who have been given eyes to see and ears to hear can perceive the redemptive picture God paints through our waiting.

In every story of righteous waiting, God has hidden the secrets of the kingdom of heaven. Your waiting is meant to be a witness not only to yourself, but to the watching world. Do you have ears to hear? Will you be a willing student in the school of waiting?

What Is God's Story?

A key to seeing your life as a parable—that is, to understand how your story is picturing God's story—is to know what God's story is. His story began before the foundation of the world and it extends into eternity. It is told in the sixty-six books of Scripture that make up the Bible. It's impossible to do the story justice in just a few pages, but here is a synopsis.

God created Adam and Eve in a good world where all of their needs were met. When they disobeyed God, sin entered the world, and along with it came death, disease, and decay. The whole earth was cursed. Each of Adam and Eve's offspring was born with the same cursed nature, so that they were drawn to sin with an irresistible attraction.

God chose one of those descendants, Abraham, and set him apart from all other people. He made three promises to Abraham: to give him offspring, to bless the nations through that offspring, and to give that offspring a land that would be theirs forever.

Throughout the generations, God added to these promises so that it became clear that God's promise to Abraham would be fulfilled not just by offspring in general, but by one very special descendant. God sent prophets to Israel (the descendants of Abraham through his grandson Jacob) who spoke of an anointed one, the Messiah, who would save his people from their sins.

At times the people of Israel believed those promises. At other times, they disbelieved them and worshiped other gods. God gave them the land of Canaan, as he had promised to Abraham, but when Israel served other gods, he took it away from them for seventy years. Even after the people of Israel returned to the land of Canaan, the prophesied child still did not appear. Finally, even the prophets went silent. The children of Abraham had been waiting for this promised offspring for nearly two thousand years.

Then, after all that time, a woman from Nazareth gave birth to a baby named Jesus. Though he looked like the ordinary son of a carpenter, he was the Son of God, the promised Messiah Israel had been waiting for. He lived on earth, healing the sick and raising the dead. And just when it seemed his ministry was taking off, the rulers of Jerusalem put him to death.

But God's plan was not thwarted. Jesus took the punishment that we deserved for our sins so that those who accept his sacrifice on their behalf will never have to face the wrath of God. It was by dying that Jesus crushed death and broke the curse of sin that Adam's descendants had lived under. He showed his power over death by rising to life again after three days. He stayed on earth for another forty days before ascending to heaven to take his place beside God the Father. He left his followers with the promise that he would return to earth and make right all that is wrong with the world. He would give them a homeland that they would never have to leave, which would be free from death and disease and decay.

We know what the end of the story will be, but we wait for it without knowing when it will come. It may come within our lifetime. No one knows the day or the hour it will come but God the Father himself.

And so we wait.

2

Waiting for a Bridegroom

Take my love, my Lord, I pour
At Thy feet its treasure store.

Frances Ridley Havergal, "Take My Life and Let it Be"

Katy has wanted to be married for as long as she can remember. Her number one career goal was always to be the mother of a large family. She read books on marriage and parenting when she was in her teens. Still unattached after college, she applied to graduate schools a bit reluctantly, worried that further study might cut into her childbearing years if the right man came along.

In spite of this, she finds herself in her midthirties with no prospect of a husband. Many of her peers who had other career aspirations had to adjust them as they married and had children, while she has the freedom to pursue any career. Any career, that is, besides the one she most wants. Sometimes it seems like our deepest desires are the ones God forgets.

It's not that she finds singleness itself so bad, but living in perpetual limbo is difficult. She says, "Life would be a lot easier if I knew that lifelong singleness is God's plan for me rather than living with uncertainty." As she's struggled to come to terms with her singleness, the question that plagues her is, If God wants her to be single, why hasn't he taken away her desire for marriage?

Some would answer the question by saying that God allows this desire to persist because he does, in fact, want Katy to be married. They suggest that if she adjusts her idea of the kind of man she's looking for, God will give her a husband. I think these people with their well-meant suggestions are missing the mark. While God may choose to bring Katy a husband any day, it's also possible that he intends for her heart to continue to desire marriage without intending to satisfy that desire with a husband.

Pictures of Desolation

Throughout the Scriptures, we find pictures of a bride without a bridegroom. In the biblical world, there's no such thing as a self-centered, *Sex and the City* single lifestyle. A bride without a bridegroom is a picture of desolation. Take Ruth. Naomi rightly discerned that there was no future in ancient Israel for a widowed Moabitess. Her widowhood consigned her to a place of poverty. God ultimately provided a husband for Ruth, but until he did, her life was one of poverty and shame.

While widowhood was common, it was highly uncommon for a woman never to marry. (There wasn't a category for "single" on ancient census forms.) Yet among the other tragic accounts in the book of Judges, we find the strange story of Jephthah's daughter in Judges 11. She was put to death because of her father's ill-considered vow. We are told that she and her friends weep, not over the fact that she will die, but that she will die a virgin. It was considered a tragedy in that society for a woman to go to her grave unmarried.

We can be grateful that the plight of an unmarried woman today is not what it would have been in ancient times. She can work and support herself. She can own property. She doesn't have to depend upon children to financially support her in old age.

Yet there is still sadness for a woman who considers that she may never give birth and never know the love of a husband. There is still shame in a society that asks "What's wrong with you?" if you never pair up with another person. In spite of the fact that these aspects of singleness are painful, I believe God has purpose in that pain.

When the Bridegroom Comes

There's another picture in the Bible of a bride without a bride-groom. Those around her who see her plight judge her forsaken. That bride was Israel. In exile, she was as desolate as a woman without a husband or children. But the prophet Isaiah proph-esied a hopeful future for Israel:

> For Zion's sake I will not keep silent,
>   and for Jerusalem's sake I will not be quiet,
> until her righteousness goes forth as brightness,
>   and her salvation as a burning torch.
> The nations shall see your righteousness,
>   and all the kings your glory,
> and you shall be called by a new name
>   that the mouth of the LORD will give.
> You shall be a crown of beauty in the hand of the LORD,
>   and a royal diadem in the hand of your God.

You shall no more be termed Forsaken,
    and your land shall no more be termed Desolate,
but you shall be called My Delight Is in Her,
    and your land Married;
for the LORD delights in you,
    and your land shall be married.
For as a young man marries a young woman,
    so shall your sons marry you,
and as the bridegroom rejoices over the bride,
    so shall your God rejoice over you. (Isa. 62:1–5)

This prophecy portrays God's return of favor to Israel as the coming of a longed-for bridegroom. It was partially fulfilled by Israel's return from exile, but was ultimately fulfilled in the coming of Jesus, who referred to himself as the Bridegroom.

Watching and Waiting as a Parable

We find yet another bride waiting for a bridegroom in Jesus's parable of the ten virgins in Matthew 25. Jesus told us that the kingdom of heaven will be like ten virgins who take lamps and go out to meet a bridegroom. That's a scenario that is not immediately familiar to those of us living in the twenty-first century. I confess that before I ever studied it, I thought it described some sort of large-scale polygamous wedding! But as any commentary will tell you, the ten virgins are not, in fact, brides. They are bridesmaids, friends of the bride who share in the joy of her wedding day.

In the Jewish society of Jesus's day, the first step of a marriage was the betrothal. This might happen while the bride was still young, and thus a significant period of time passed between betrothal and marriage. Once the day finally arrived for the wedding to take place, the groom would go to the house of the bride to get her. The whole wedding party would then joyfully process through the torch-lit night from the bride's house to that of the bridegroom. Once they arrived, the groom would host the wedding feast.

In this parable, the groom was delayed. We are not told why he was delayed, and the members of the waiting wedding party apparently didn't know either. As far as they knew, he might arrive at any minute, or he might keep them waiting for hours. Their wait lasted longer than they expected, and they naturally fell asleep.

The waiting—and the sleeping—of the bridal party abruptly ended in the middle of the night when word came that the bridegroom had finally arrived. Five of the bridesmaids had plenty of oil and were ready to start the procession. The five who had burned all of their oil started to scramble, but they could not find more oil in time to be welcomed into the feast with the bridal procession.

It is important to note that all ten of the girls fell asleep, not just the foolish ones. Although this parable is about watching, *watching* here is not synonymous with wakefulness but readiness. The wise maidens could sleep because they were prepared and would be ready the moment they were awakened by the bridegroom. The foolish maidens slept through the hours in which they might have found more oil.

It is similar to the difference between sleeping peacefully the night before a vacation because you are packed and ready, and getting caught unprepared for a trip because you accidentally fell asleep. The foolish virgins have slept away the time of preparation, so they missed the bridal procession and were not allowed to enter the feast.

This parable illustrates several truths about the kingdom of heaven. First, although Christ's kingdom has begun, it has not yet been fully realized. In this sense, we are like a bride betrothed but not yet married. The consummation of the kingdom will occur when Jesus returns in power and triumph. Like the wedding party in the parable, we don't know how long it will be before our Bridegroom returns to claim his bride.

Second, if we want to be ready for that consummation when the kingdom comes, we must be fortified for a long wait. In spite of the delay, we must keep our bags packed. The waiting will end suddenly, and we must not allow the waiting to make us forget what we are ultimately waiting for. In the words of German theologian Helmut Thielicke:

> With Jesus we do not know when he will come again or when he will summon us to come with him. We do not know the moment when everything that is so madly important to us—our career, our success, our failure, and our dejection—will vanish. We do not know when he will become the only thing that has any importance to us. Therefore we must be on the lookout and ready for him at any moment. For every single hour of our life is marked with this one, unpredictable moment when we shall stand alone and face Jesus Christ.[4]

The Waiting Church

We've looked at several different biblical scenarios: the tragic daughter of Jepthah, weeping that she will die a virgin; desolate Israel, a husbandless bride whose weeping is turned to joy when the bridegroom returns; and the bridesmaids who have not prepared for the bridegroom's arrival and are caught unawares when he finally comes. Which story will be Katy's story?

If God ever gives her a husband, she will live out the picture Isaiah foretold of rejoicing in the long-awaited bridegroom. Her wedding and the feast that follows will foreshadow the marriage supper of the Lamb described in Revelation. She will be able to look back on her season of singleness with gratitude that comes with hindsight.

But what if she never marries? Does she fail as a picture of the gospel? Not at all. Instead, she will live and die as a portrait of what the church is meant to be now. Jesus forewarned that there would be a time between his ascension and his return, a time of waiting on the promised Bridegroom:

> Now John's disciples and the Pharisees were fasting. And people came and said to [Jesus], "Why do John's disciples and the disciples of the Pharisees fast, but your disciples do not fast?" And Jesus said to them, "Can the wedding guests fast while the bridegroom is with them? As long as they have the bridegroom with them, they cannot fast. The days will come when the bridegroom is taken away from them, and then they will fast in that day." (Mark 2:18–20)

We are living in the day Jesus described. So what does the fasting he predicted look like? While we might not immediately recognize celibacy within the single life as a form of fasting, we should. A single Christian living by God's commands does not have a sex life, and this is a hardship! By God's grace, Katy will fast from sex until he brings her a husband. She will also fast from a lot of other comforts that come with marriage (along with the attendant trials). And if she dies without ever becoming one flesh with another person, she will die in the company of the faithful ones described in Hebrews 11 who didn't receive the thing they waited for, but who believed that God rewards those who seek him.

This same hope can characterize those who never expect to marry. Many Christians who experience same-sex attraction face the prospect of a lifelong fast from sexual intimacy. The Bible teaches that sex is meant only for marriage between a man and a woman, and any other means of satisfying one's sexual desires is immorality.[5] There's no such thing as God-sanctioned same-sex marriage. If you are attracted to others of your sex and have no hope for marriage in this life, there is every hope that you will be satisfied fully and completely in the life to come. Though the world may scoff at your self-denial, you can know that there is something better in store for you than any sexual relationship on this earth. Jesus lived a full and complete human life, but he never experienced marriage or sexual intimacy. We too can fast from these things if God calls us to because there is great joy set before us when we will be united to him forever.

Loneliness of body and spirit are hardships, but they don't have to be hardships suffered in vain. Sometimes it's difficult to see the purpose of days and years of loneliness, but we don't have to see the point of them to trust God with them. Elisabeth Elliot makes a case for giving your loneliness to God:

> God gives us material for sacrifice. Sometimes the sacrifice makes little sense to others, but when offered to Him is always accepted. What was the "point" in God's asking Abraham for the sacrifice of his beloved son, Isaac? . . . Our offerings to Him may very likely be seen as senseless or even fanatical, but He receives them. Jesus received the precious ointment from the worshiping woman, although those present thought it a foolish waste. It is a lesson I understood very dimly in 1948, but it has become clearer and clearer the further I go with God. I have tried to explain it sometimes to people who are lonely and longing for love. "Give it to Jesus," I say. The loneliness itself is material for sacrifice.

The very longings themselves can be offered to Him who understands perfectly. The transformation into something He can use for the good of others takes place only when the offering is put into His hands.

What will He do with these offerings? Never mind. He knows what to do.[6]

Our Father is trustworthy. Whether you hope for marriage in this life or not, if you are living for the world to come, God can use your story to point others toward the feast to end all fasting, when our heavenly Bridegroom appears.

Holy Discontentment

If you are a Christian with a desire for marriage, the chances are good that someone has quoted to you Psalm 37:4: "Delight yourself in the LORD, and he will give you the desires of your heart." People have used this verse to assure single women that if marriage is the desire of their hearts, then God has a husband picked out for them.

Upon a closer reading, it is obvious that this verse does not mean God will give you or me everything we've desired. This is a conditional promise. In order to receive the desires of your heart, you must delight yourself in the Lord. If you are delighting yourself in the Lord, what is the desire of your heart? He is.

While this verse may not promise an earthly end to your singleness, it does give you hope for joy in the Lord. Does this mean that you should be content with your singleness? I would answer that while you may never be content *with* your singleness, you can know God's joy *in* your singleness. You shouldn't feel guilty that you still desire marriage. In fact, it should be for you and those around you a parable of the holy discontentment we should feel until Christ returns.

Waiting Well While Waiting for a Bridegroom

The Bible tells us that we are aliens and strangers in this world. A single person knows what it feels like to live as an "odd man out" in a couples' world. Why not glorify God by acknowledging that alienation while asking him to make you less at home in the world?

When I was still single, it was hard to remember that married people might also feel lonely or transient or unsettled or any of the states I associated with my singleness. But the truth is, we all feel these things. Unfortunately, we too often wait for someone else to see our emptiness and fill it out of their fullness.

Whenever I was able to see beyond my own loneliness to someone else's, God would begin to work. When I focused on a need that wasn't my own, the pain of being alone would start to subside. Someone who lives with unmet desires is uniquely able to identify with and comfort others who live with unmet desires, even if their longings are of a different sort. If we wait to reach out to others from a position of fullness, we will never do it. If, on the other hand, we love others out of our own emptiness, we will—paradoxically—find we have an abundance of love to give.

Another way that you can wait well while waiting for a bridegroom is to live a life that stands in stark contrast to our cultural idol of sexual fulfillment. The world tells us that life without sex is not worth living. It tells us that whatever your sexual proclivity may be, it is essential to the pursuit of happiness that you have means to practice it. But God, the Creator of our bodies, has a very different message for us in his Word, which says, "The body is not meant for sexual immorality, but for the Lord, and the Lord for the body" (1 Cor. 6:13b).

Why not live a chaste life with the knowledge that you are embodying God's will for his church as we fast and wait for our

Bridegroom? Why not continue to pray for a spouse, even as you join in the words of the Spirit and the bride who cry, "Come, Lord Jesus!" (Rev. 22:20)?

Ready and Waiting

When America went to war after Pearl Harbor, many couples married rapidly as men were drafted into the armed forces. I have a friend whose mother, a young woman at the time, became engaged to her beau who subsequently shipped out with the Navy before they could have a wedding. They weren't able to marry until he had enough leave to come home. She and her mother planned the wedding down to the last detail. They even printed the wedding invitations, but they left the date off. They didn't know when the bridegroom would be able to make it, so they waited at the ready. Finally, after eighteen long months, a telegram came that said, "You should get the white dress you've been wanting." The groom was on his way! They wrote in the date by hand and sent off the invitations.

We know who our Bridegroom is; we just don't know when he's going to appear. Like the girl waiting for her fiancé to get leave and come home to marry her, there is much we can do to get ready for Jesus's return. While she may have spent her time packing her trousseau into trunks, we should spend ours laying up treasure in heaven (Matt. 6:20). As she tore into his letters, eager to know about the man she loved, we should pore over God's Word, reminding ourselves of why he is worth waiting for. As she resisted the overtures of any other man, we must guard our hearts from idols, keeping them pure and devoted to Jesus alone as we wait for his appearing. God has not promised every one of his daughters an earthly bridegroom, but none who watch and wait for a heavenly Bridegroom will be disappointed.

3

Waiting for a Child

Three things are never satisfied;
four never say, "Enough":
Sheol, the barren womb,
the land never satisfied with water,
and the fire that never says, "Enough."

Proverbs 30:15b–16

Christine and Paul married when she was in her late twenties and he was in his midthirties. Christine had trouble conceiving, and doctors determined that she suffered from endometriosis. After surgery, she started fertility treatments. She and Paul were overjoyed when they discovered Christine was pregnant. They soared on the elation of years of pent-up hope and longing.

Their hopes crashed when Christine suffered a miscarriage. Devastated, for months Christine kept the ultrasound picture tucked inside her shirt next to her heart. They continued with infertility treatment, though month after month passed without another pregnancy. Christine struggled spiritually as she waited. She recalls, "I loved the Lord; I knew he had a providentially designed sovereign plan for my life, but I struggled with the fact that we were praying for a noble desire, and it was going unanswered. I would pray, face down on the floor, crying and pleading for God to allow me to conceive."

After several years, they started looking into adoption, though they still hoped to conceive. Christine's endometriosis grew worse and became very painful. Her doctors eventually recommended a total hysterectomy. Christine and Paul put off the needed operation that they knew would end their hope of biological children. After another year passed, Christine finally underwent the hysterectomy. Before the surgery, Christine had to sign a paper acknowledging that she would never be able to bear a child. She told me, "Putting pen to that paper is a moment I'll never forget. It was so solemn and final, like a prison door clanking behind me."

After her surgery, with the hope of conception now ended, Christine and Paul's quest to adopt a child took on a feeling of desperation. They made a video of their home, hoping to be chosen by potential birth mothers. Their wait stretched on without much communication from the adoption agency. It felt like everyone else around them had a child. Christine's emotions were so raw that she avoided baby showers and would even change the channel if an ad for baby products came on television.

Seventeen months after the hysterectomy, Christine and Paul learned that they had been chosen to be the adoptive parents for a set of fraternal twins. Tragically, the birth mother went into premature labor, and the baby girl died at birth. Then the mother changed her mind about the adoption and chose to keep the baby boy. So the waiting stretched on.

Several months later, they learned that they had been chosen by a mother who had already delivered. Instant parents, they picked up their new baby girl from the hospital and took her back to a hotel room. After three days of bliss with the baby, they learned that her birth mother had changed her mind. Because of the state's revocation rights period, Christine and Paul had no choice but to take the beautiful baby girl back to the adoption agency and say goodbye to her forever.

With this fresh heartbreak, Christine began to question God. Her deepest fear was that she would never have a child. She spent months in the book of Habakkuk, asking with the prophet, "O Lord, how long?" (1:2).

Infertility and Shame

In every era, infertility has brought with it not only heartbreak, but painful cultural shame. In ancient times, offspring were a sign of bounty and blessing. Children could work the land, care for their parents, and defend the family's honor. Couples who had no children were assumed to have displeased the gods. This is why pagan tribal religions are woven through with fertility rituals. The woman with a closed womb felt that she had to appease the gods and earn their favor in order to bear a child.

While few people hold this belief today, they can still perpetuate a stigma of blame in the remarks they make to infertile couples. Even though they may have good intentions, people who tell infertile couples to "just relax and stop trying so hard" imply that infertility is the couple's fault. People who complain about surprise babies or suggest "there must be something in the water" whenever new pregnancies are announced unintentionally increase the stigma felt by those who are desperate to conceive. While it may seem like the most sensitive approach to an infertile couple to downplay the blessing of children, it is actually more painful for struggling couples to be around people who don't seem to remember that children are a precious gift.

In addition to the shame that may come from insensitive comments, the infertile woman may ruthlessly blame herself. If miscarriage has been a part of her ordeal, she may obsess over what she might have done that caused it. While Internet research is a helpful tool for tips on a healthy pregnancy, when a mother's child has died in her womb, all those recommendations can sound like accusations.

As Christians, we sometimes compound the perceived shame of infertility by suggesting that it has a spiritual root. A lack of children is no indication that a couple is spiritually undeserving. We are *all* spiritually undeserving; if God waited to give children until a couple was perfectly prepared or content, the human race would die out. Barren women may feel condemned because they are grieving their lack of children instead of cheerfully accepting it as God's will. In much helpful and well-meant advice, what the infertile couple often hears is the message that "God is denying you children because you haven't learned your lesson. If you could just be more content in him, God would give you a child."

The Barren Matriarch

If someone had written the story of Abraham and Sarah's marriage, it might have read something like an ancient version of Christine and Paul's. The Bible doesn't tell us about Sarah's disappointment month after month, year after year, when she failed to conceive. Although she didn't have modern-day fertility treatments at her disposal, there were plenty of superstitions and folk remedies for conception. Sarah must have tried all of them, but she continued on childless until she was past the age of childbearing.

Perhaps once they knew there was no longer any hope of bearing a child, Sarah and Abraham were able to grieve and move on. Sarah didn't have to weep afresh each month. Abraham chose his steward, a man named Eliezer of Damascus, to be his heir. But then God reopened the wound by promising to make Abraham the father of many nations by giving him a son (Gen. 15:4).

Abraham believed God's promise, though he didn't know how God would accomplish it, given that his wife was past her childbearing years. After the promise, Sarah's desire for a child seems to have taken on a renewed desperation. Determined to get children for Abraham, she chose her still-fertile maidservant to be her surrogate, to sleep with Abraham and bear him offspring.

Sarah's plan to circumvent her own barrenness was not God's plan to fulfill his promise. He intended to give the barren woman a child born from her own womb. It took Sarah a while to understand this, and her attempt at taking matters into her own hands caused harm to her husband, her maidservant, and her maidservant's child. But God does not reserve children for those who deserve them. In spite of Sarah's sin, God kept his promise, and Sarah gave birth to Isaac when she was over ninety years old.

Why did God make Abraham and Sarah wait? Why did he give them a child in their old age rather than when they were young and vigorous? Abraham's wait for his promised offspring became an emblem of the wait of all of his descendants for the ultimate promised offspring. Isaac's birth wasn't the final fulfillment of the covenant; it was only the start of it. God's chosen people would wait for generations before the Messiah, the Savior of Israel, was born.

The writer of Hebrews does not emphasize Sarah's doubt that God would give her offspring, but the belief that won out in the end: "By faith Sarah herself received power to conceive, even when she was past the age, since she considered him faithful who had promised" (Heb. 11:11). She was an example to generations of Israelites who would endure slavery, wilderness, and exile. The people of Israel were not meant to give up on God's covenant—to grieve and move on—but to keep hoping in faith, even though keeping hope alive could be painful.

Pain as a Parable

Infertility is like a wound that gets opened every month. There is hope of healing the wound by conceiving a child. There is also the potential that the pain will go away if buried under thick scars. A barren woman may be tempted to harden her heart so that it won't keep getting broken. She may close herself off from her husband so that she doesn't have to see his pain and share her own. She may become bitter, calloused, and scornful of those who enjoy what she has been denied, so that she doesn't have to live day after day in the raw pain of unmet desire.

This temptation must be fervently resisted. We must not be like Sarah, who protected herself with cynicism (Gen. 18:12–14). We must be Hannahs, allowing our grief and longing to prostrate us before God (1 Samuel 1). Hannah's longing moved her to prayer. Her prayers produced a prophet for a son, one who would crown David king of Israel. Not every prayer, even if it is as heartfelt as Hannah's, will lead to a child. But Hannah's willingness to own her pain, to pour it out before the Lord and admit it to Eli, found favor with God. We should emulate her humility, expecting similar favor, even though we are not promised that God's favor will be manifest in a child.

Contentment and grief are not incompatible states. Just as we weep over violence and death and sin, it is appropriate to weep over a womb that has not born a child. All is not as it should be. The pain of infertility should send us deep into the goodness of God for comfort. You can find contentment in the mercies of a tender Father as you grieve the barrenness of your womb.

Grieving at the brokenness of this world points beyond to the life to come. If all our desires were satisfied here, why would we want Christ to return and establish his kingdom? Though we live in a fallen world, those who have lacked children in this life have much to look forward to in the world to come.

The Prayers of Israel

Elizabeth's story closely resembles Sarah's. We meet her in the opening pages of the book of Luke. She and her husband, the priest Zechariah, have no children because she is barren. Luke makes clear to the reader that their childlessness is not a result of unfaithfulness or sin: "And they were both righteous before God, walking blamelessly in all the commandments and statutes of the Lord" (Luke 1:6). While they had their own years of painful waiting, they have now aged past hope.

No doubt Zechariah and Elizabeth prayed for years that God would remove their barrenness, and with it the stigma that came to children of the covenant with no offspring. When the angel Gabriel appears to Zechariah, the first thing he says is, "Do not be afraid, Zechariah, for your prayers have been heard, and your wife Elizabeth will bear you a son" (Luke 1:13). On one level, the birth of John the Baptist was the answer to a specific and private prayer of a childless couple. This is how Elizabeth interprets her son's conception; she says, "Thus the Lord has done for me in the days when he looked on me, to take away my reproach among people" (Luke 1:25). She sees a narrow and personal answer to her own prayer, and she is right.

But this is not the only correct interpretation of Gabriel's announcement. There is a wider purpose of God at work. It is not just Zechariah's prayer that has been answered, but the prayers of all Israel!

The setting for Gabriel's announcement is very important. Zechariah was fulfilling his priestly duty of burning incense before the Lord. The priest offering incense was chosen by lot, and we know from Jewish writings that a priest was only permitted the privilege once in a lifetime. The temple was the center of worship for the people of Israel where they came to offer sacrifices and pray for the redemption of Israel. The prayer most dear to the heart of any faithful child of Israel was the coming of the promised Messiah. In his role as priest, Zechariah functioned as chief intercessor for God's people. While he prayed, Luke reminds us that the crowd outside was also praying (v. 10).

Priests had been offering incense for hundreds of years. Multitudes outside the temple had been waiting for the Messiah for generations. After all that waiting, all that longing, the word was spoken, "your prayers have been heard" (v. 13). The shame of Israel would be removed! The child Zechariah's wife would bear would be a herald, announcing the coming of the Holy One of Israel, the promised Messiah. Israel would no longer appear before the nations as one who stood forgotten by her God. The birth of baby John, forerunner of Jesus, was the result of personal, private prayers as well as the fulfillment of prophecy and years of corporate prayer. Just as God had fulfilled his covenant by giving a baby to Abraham and Sarah in their old age, after a very long wait, God was giving Israel the child he had promised.

God's Promise to the Childless

Our God is a kind God. When he removes barrenness, he reveals the generosity at the core of his character: "He gives the barren woman a home, making her the joyous mother of children" (Ps. 113:9a). Perhaps you feel that by denying you children, God is showing himself to be unkind, but we mustn't confuse delay with denial. I didn't fall in love until I was thirty-three. For me, the joy of love was not denied but delayed. The delay made the delight all the sweeter when it finally came. While God has not promised to give you children in this life, if you are a believer, he has promised to remove your barrenness in the life to come.

I love the scene that the prophet Isaiah paints of the formerly barren woman, now fruitful in the new creation:

"Sing, O barren one, who did not bear;
    break forth into singing and cry aloud,
    you who have not been in labor!
For the children of the desolate one will be more
    than the children of her who is married," says
        the LORD.
"Enlarge the place of your tent,
    and let the curtains of your habitations be
        stretched out;
do not hold back; lengthen your cords
    and strengthen your stakes.
For you will spread abroad to the right and to the left,
    and your offspring will possess the nations
    and will people the desolate cities." (Isa. 54:1–3)

45

This woman who has been all alone now has a tent bulging with offspring. It is so full that she has to reinforce the tent pegs. Not only is she going to find herself with lots of children, they are going to be victorious offspring, ruling over other nations. The same thing is portrayed in Isaiah 49:21 when a mother who has been bereaved with no offspring is shocked to find herself the mother of many.

This prophecy has fulfillment on several levels. First, it reminds Israel that all her numerous descendants came from a barren woman. Sarah was no longer capable of having children, yet God opened her womb and made her the mother of his chosen people. Nevertheless, at the time Isaiah spoke, the people of God were a barren people because Israel had not yet produced the promised Messiah. The coming of Christ was one fulfillment of this prophecy because he removed the curse of spiritual barrenness from Israel. His kingdom expands not through natural offspring but by those who are born again in him.

It also has a future dimension in which every kind of barrenness will cease when Christ returns. There will be no infertility in the new heaven and the new earth. We sow the seeds of the offspring that will fill that tent when we raise up spiritual children.

Spiritual Offspring

When we nurture faith in the lives of others, we rear spiritual offspring. Sometimes that means playing a part in someone's spiritual birth through evangelism. Other times it means training them up in the faith through teaching and discipleship.

When I suggest that God may remove your barrenness by giving you spiritual children, your instinct may be to respond, "No, thank you, I'll take the real thing." I understand that kind of thinking. It is the same for the unmarried woman who finds the promise of Christ as her spiritual Bridegroom to be small comfort. But just because a spiritual child seems less real to us than a biological or adopted child does not make it true. When we exalt the earthly over the eternal, we favor the shadow over the thing it represents. While the object itself may be out of your view and thus intangible, it is in fact every bit as real as its shadow.

Our minds are conditioned to believe that what is most real is that which can be seen and touched. The Bible presents a very different framework for reality. Paul writes, "For the things that are seen are transient, but the things that are unseen are eternal" (2 Cor. 4:18b). As Christians, we are those who hope for what we do not see (Rom. 8:24). While it may be hard to imagine gleaning the same satisfaction by having spiritual offspring, I've no doubt that on the other side of eternity, your joy will be so complete that you won't feel even a hint of wistfulness for experiences you missed in this life.

Waiting Well While Waiting for a Child

When infertility causes you to cry, "O LORD, how long?" remember, that is the question that God's people have always been asking (Hab. 1:2). The people of Israel asked "How long?" as they waited for the Messiah. We now ask, "How long?" as we wait for the new heavens and the new (fertile) earth.

We don't have to wait idly for that day; we can prepare for it by raising up spiritual offspring. There are many ways to nurture spiritual children in this life. You may do it by teaching Sunday school. You may have spiritual children by serving as a foster parent. You may sponsor an orphan overseas, not merely sending money for physical needs, but also praying for your child daily. You could serve as a mentor for a teenager from a troubled home. You can use the time and energy and money that you would spend on children to build God's kingdom.

These relationships will not necessarily have an earthly payoff. Some of them may lead to lasting ties and a mutually rewarding relationship, but others may simply take without ever giving back. Some may break your heart, just as earthly children do at times. Even so, we should heed Jesus's teaching that we should give to those who cannot repay us, "for you will be repaid at the resurrection of the just" (Luke 14:14). As you become a spiritual mother with spiritual children and grandchildren, you can look forward to the bulging tent prophesied by Isaiah. This requires believing by faith that spiritual children are real children and that investment in the life to come brings a good return.

If you are reading this book and you have children, you should be equally compelled to seek spiritual offspring. This may primarily happen as you disciple the children you are raising, but it doesn't have to end there. Your children need to see the family of God as their true family, and you can encourage this by investing in the lives of others.

I want to encourage you who have earthly offspring to seek to involve childless Christian adults in the life of your family. Invite mature single believers into your home to spend time with your children, not as babysitters, but as godly examples. When I was single and without any idea whether I would ever have children, it was extremely meaningful to me when some friends asked me to be a godmother for their daughter. This may not be a tradition familiar to you, and in some circles it is a role chiefly associated with the giving of presents, but the role is meant to be a spiritual one. In agreeing to be a godmother, I committed to pray for my goddaughter and take an active role in her spiritual life. It was a strong reminder to me that, though childless, I was not exempt from spiritual offspring.

Your spiritual children may or may not have the same last name as you, but I hope they will be so central to your life that you will be able to say with the apostle John, "I have no greater joy than to hear that my children are walking in the truth" (3 John 4).

An Everlasting Answer

Christine and Paul's story has a happy ending. After many years of waiting and disappointment, they adopted a beautiful son. "The joyful emotion once we held our son defies my best ability to capture it with words," Christine recalls. "My heart sang, I felt lighter, all my senses were heightened, and it was like nothing I've ever experienced before. God had heard our prayers."

Christine's words echo the words that Gabriel spoke to Zechariah: "Your prayer has been heard" (Luke 1:13). Her prayer for a child has been answered in this life. Some barren women will have to wait to see their barrenness removed in the life to come, but they can anticipate that day by nurturing spiritual children. For that to be a consolation, you must fix your eyes not on what is seen here, but on what is unseen and eternal. The end of barrenness will be more real than any pain felt in our fleeting time on this earth, and the joy that comes with it will go on and on forever and ever and ever.

4

Waiting for Healing

God uses chronic pain and weakness, along with other afflictions, as his chisel for sculpting our lives. Felt weakness deepens dependence on Christ for strength each day. The weaker we feel, the harder we lean.

J. I. Packer, God's Plans for You

Tim was diagnosed with stage-four colon cancer at twenty-nine years old. When his doctors determined the extent of the cancer through exploratory surgery, they sewed him back up and told his wife, Annie, to get their affairs in order. They didn't expect Tim to survive more than a few months.

The doctors were wrong, as they so often are. In part, they underestimated Tim's determination to fight his cancer. A West Point graduate and former US Army Airborne Ranger, Tim approached cancer treatment with the same steely will to survive that he would have employed had he been captured by an enemy of the state. Over the next sixteen years, the cancer returned four times, and each time the treatment was more grueling. I'm pretty sure that by the time he had endured twenty-nine surgeries and the ferocious side effects of five protocols of chemotherapy, he would have preferred to be tortured by a human enemy.

For sixteen years, Tim and Annie lived with the shadow of Tim's death looming over them. But they lived, and they lived well. When Tim's cancer was first diagnosed, their daughter was just ten months old. After the first round of treatment, doctors told them that fathering more children would be a physical impossibility for Tim. Yet to the complete disbelief of his oncologists, a few years later Annie became pregnant and gave birth to a healthy son. Tim approached parenting with earnest intentionality, aware that his time with his children might be short. The desire for them to grow up knowing their father spurred him on to fight for his life.

Each time Tim went into surgery, Annie would read Psalm 27 to him. The psalm ends, "I believe that I shall look upon the goodness of the LORD in the land of the living! Wait for the LORD; be strong, and let your heart take courage; wait for the LORD!" Tim was trying as hard as humanly possible to survive his cancer. Yet his ultimate hope was not in the doctor's skill, but in the sure knowledge that his suffering would end one day in eternal life, which can never be threatened by cancer. He could say with the apostle Paul, "Christ will be honored in my body, whether by life or by death. For to me to live is Christ, and to die is gain. If I am to live in the flesh, that means fruitful labor for me. Yet which I shall choose I cannot tell. I am hard pressed between the two. My desire is to depart and be with Christ, for that is far better. But to remain in the flesh is more necessary on your account" (Phil. 1:20b–24).

Tim had to learn to live with a dual focus; one eye looked

forward to the end of his suffering while the other focused on faithful living in the midst of suffering. Much of Tim and Annie's time, energy, and money was spent fighting Tim's cancer. Even as they prayed for healing and pursued medical treatment, Tim longed for the full and complete healing that he knew would come with a resurrected body. Only the prospect of heaven allowed him to face his terminal diagnosis with hope. Only the sustaining grace of God gave him the strength to keep putting one foot in front of the other while he lived in a body ravaged by cancer.

Tim could have used his illness as an excuse to withdraw from leadership and service to the church. The knowledge that his life would likely be cut short could have been a justification for living for himself. But Tim actively served God's people. He was an elder in their church, and he and Annie helped lead the singles group. They were deeply invested in the lives of others and spent copious time in one-on-one discipleship and pre-marital counseling sessions. I was a member of their home group, which Tim continued to lead even while going through chemotherapy. I remember sitting at a kitchen table with Tim as he helped me decide how to choose a curriculum for a women's small group. Because his six-foot-five frame was gaunt from chemo, it was no exaggeration to say he looked like he had been in a concentration camp. His mouth was full of sores, but he slowly and deliberately extolled the merits of *The Pilgrim's Progress* for group study.

Most of us wouldn't have the kind of physical stamina and endurance Tim did (I know I don't), and I'm not suggesting everyone with a terminal illness should maintain the levels of activity that he did. But Tim's physical endurance was an inspiration to me whenever I sought spiritual and emotional endurance. If something seemed beyond my strength, I would think, Tim gets out of bed every morning in the strength of the Lord. Surely I can face my own trials in the strength of the same Lord.

Tim loved his family and his church to the end. When his body finally failed, around seven hundred people turned out for the memorial service. A friend of his read a letter Tim had written for the service in which he said, "I've prayed to live, but God is telling me that he has something BETTER in store for me, which I'm already experiencing at this moment. It would be wonderful to hear all the nice things said about me at the memorial service. But there is only one thing I want to hear. But that is only audible on the other side of eternity, 'Well done, my good and faithful servant.'"

Groaning in Tents

I am not a camper. The few times that I've attempted to rough it and sleep outside, about ten o'clock, I start asking myself, "Now, why am I doing this?" I hate the thought that my perfectly comfortable bed at home lies empty while I'm in a sleeping bag on the ground. For me, a tent is not an acceptable substitute for home.

In 2 Corinthians 5:1–3, Paul describes our bodies as earthly tents, a place to reside only until we receive everlasting bodies in our heavenly home:

> For we know that if the tent that is our earthly home is destroyed, we have a building from God, a house not made with hands, eternal in the heavens. For in this tent we groan, longing to put on our heavenly dwelling, if indeed by putting it on we may not be found naked.

The world stops feeling like a comfortable place when our bodies attack themselves. Even a minor sickness can remind us that our bodies are not permanent homes. When sickness enters our lives, we become keenly aware that our world is fallen. Our bodies are a gift from God, but as they age and get sick, they cause a lot of groaning.

While sickness, like death, is a product of the fall and therefore not a good thing in itself, it has the good by-product of helping us to feel less at home in the world. When we aren't at home in our bodies, it reminds us that "our citizenship is in heaven, and from it we await a Savior, the Lord Jesus Christ, who will transform our lowly body to be like his glorious body, by the power that enables him even to subject all things to himself" (Phil. 3:20–21). Illness is not something that we should embrace for its own sake, but we can celebrate the fact that it makes us long for our heavenly home and resurrected bodies, in the same way that sleeping on the cold hard ground made me long for my bed at home.

The Hope of Healing

When sickness is serious, it is rarely over quickly. Thus, waiting is integral to the experience of illness. We wait on test results. We wait on remission. We wait on relief from side effects. Most of all, we wait on healing, and often we don't know whether that healing will come in this life or the next.

God does not always respond to prayers for healing in the same way. Sometimes he heals quickly, either through medicine or through miracles with no scientific explanation. Sometimes he heals after many months or years. Other times, God withholds healing. I have seen each of these responses to my own prayers for the healing of others. And in Scripture, we see clear examples of God acting in these different ways in response to sickness.

Luke 4 contains the kind of healing that we would all choose for ourselves and those we love. Simon Peter's mother-in-law has been stricken with a high fever. Those in the house "[appeal] to Jesus on her behalf," which basically means they offered an in-person prayer for healing. Luke tells us that Jesus "stood over her and rebuked the fever, and it left her, and immediately she rose and began to serve them" (Luke 4:39). The healing was miraculous and instantaneous. That same night, Jesus laid hands on many others and healed them.

This is the kind of healing our bodies and souls long for, the touch of our Savior that instantly restores. That kind of healing brings glory to God because it shows his miraculous power. But God is also glorified when we continue to walk in faith though we have not been healed. Anyone would praise God for instantaneous healing; there's nothing supernatural about being glad for good health. But those who praise God in the midst of their suffering, even though he has not removed that suffering, show a kind of faith that can only be attributed to the Holy Spirit within them. It is not natural to give thanks and rejoice while being imprisoned in a groaning, aching body.

When God Doesn't Heal

While Jesus healed scores of people during his time on earth, there was a particularly notable episode when he chose not to heal. Mary, Martha, and Lazarus were Jesus's close friends, so naturally the sisters sent for him when their brother became ill. Instead of rushing to their home in Bethany, Jesus waited two days before he went to Lazarus, telling his disciples, "This illness does not lead to death. It is for the glory of God, so that the Son of God may be glorified through it" (John 11:4).

This statement probably made perfect sense to the disciples.

They were accustomed to Jesus bringing glory to God by healing. It sounded like Jesus had a plan to heal Lazarus and keep him from dying. But that was not his plan. Instead, Jesus waited until he knew that Lazarus had died before going to Bethany. Suddenly, his statement about this illness not leading to death no longer made sense. In fact, it seemed *false*.

Jesus wept with Mary and Martha beside Lazarus's tomb. In the eyes of the onlookers, he must have looked like someone who had nothing to offer but compassion. This was perhaps the greatest test of faith the disciples had yet faced. When the people of Bethany saw Jesus weeping, they asked, "Could not he who opened the eyes of the blind man also have kept this man from dying?" (John 11:37b).

The answer to their question is a resounding yes, but Jesus had an even greater plan than healing Lazarus. Even so, his sorrow and compassion for Martha and Mary were genuine. This story shows that God knows our sorrows and feels them, even when he knows he's doing something better than we know. If you are waiting for God to heal you, you can trust that even if he hasn't yet answered that prayer, he sees and feels your suffering. Jesus knew that in a few moments, Mary and Martha would have their brother back, but still he wept with them.

After Jesus wept, he got to work. He commanded the stone to be removed from the tomb, against Martha's protestations. He prayed aloud, then cried out, "Lazarus, come out" (v. 43). When the Son of God speaks, even the dead must obey his voice. Lazarus, the man who had been dead for four days, walked out of his tomb.

The thing that is so satisfying about this story is that we get to see God's purpose behind what initially looked like either a lack of compassion or a lack of power. Jesus did not prevent

Lazarus's death, but he didn't let the sickness end in death. When someone is healed, there's always the possibility of a medical explanation that happened to coincide with a prayer for healing. But there's no possibility of medically explaining resurrection after four days of death! Jesus showed greater power by raising Lazarus than he would have even by healing him.

A Story of Prolonged Illness

The woman Jesus encountered in Mark 5 suffered much longer than Simon Peter's mother-in-law or Lazarus. She had been bleeding for twelve years. Any woman can imagine the misery this condition would bring. In addition to the attendant discomfort and exhaustion, it may have kept her from conceiving children. This woman had spent all her money on doctors, and they only made the problem worse. Even more devastating for an Israelite, her bleeding meant that she was perpetually unclean (Lev. 15:25). Anything she touched would become defiled, which is why it is so shocking that she touched Jesus.

Nevertheless, when this woman reached out and touched Jesus's robe, she didn't make him unclean. Instead, his purity made her pure. She could tell immediately that she was healed. The misery that had followed her for twelve years was over.

There is more to this healing than the end of this poor woman's physical suffering, wonderful as it is. In taking away her illness, Jesus also removed her uncleanness. Jesus was not defiled by touching an unclean person. It's as if water suddenly flowed uphill. Only Jesus can reverse the flow of defilement.

Consequently, this miracle serves as a powerful picture of the cleansing from sin that comes when we put our faith in Jesus. Like this woman, Israel had been helplessly unclean for hundreds of years. The prophet Isaiah had commanded the people of Judah, "Wash yourselves; make yourselves clean; remove the evil of your deeds from before my eyes; cease to do evil" (Isa. 1:5–16), but Israel had never managed to remove her own uncleanness. Now, we see that Jesus has come to fulfill the second half of Isaiah's prophecy: "Come now, let us reason together, says the LORD: though your sins are like scarlet, they shall be as white as snow; though they are red like crimson, they shall become like wool" (Isa. 1:18).

If this woman's suffering hadn't been prolonged, she would not have been such a powerful sign of the redemption that had come to Israel. She didn't choose to be ill, but she did choose to respond in faith when she met the One who could heal both her body and her soul. Her life became a parable, just as instructive as the fictional parables Jesus told. Like this woman, the people of Israel had been waiting for Jesus. They could not heal themselves. Jesus had come to take away Israel's uncleanness by forgiving her sins, but the people of Israel would have to come to him in faith. Though we cannot reach out and touch Jesus's robe, we can respond to him with the same faith the woman showed.

Waiting Well While Waiting for Healing

What does it mean to wait well when you long to be healed? Waiting well involves praying for healing and seeking a cure through medical means. It also means recognizing that God may have purposes for delaying that healing. One purpose may be to remind the healthy people around you that our bodies don't last forever. Tents are not meant to be permanent.

We all long for the restoration that will come when God gives us new, resurrected bodies. We don't have those bodies yet. Until we do, we are "those who have not seen, and yet have believed" (John 20:29). Just as the woman with the hemorrhage of blood was a living parable of Israel's need for cleansing, so those who suffer in the body serve as a parable of our need for resurrection.

How might this happen? If you suffer from a terminal illness, your life is living evidence of Psalm 103:15–17:

> As for man, his days are like grass;
> > he flourishes like a flower of the field;
> for the wind passes over it, and it is gone,
> > and its place knows it no more.
> But the steadfast love of the LORD is from everlasting to
> > everlasting on those who fear him.

Those who see you will be reminded that we are not promised long lives. Neither our health nor our continued existence on earth is guaranteed; only God's love for those who fear him endures eternally. Ultimately, we all have a terminal diagnosis and must repent before it is too late. As you wait for healing, realizing that it may not come this side of Jordan, you can help people see their urgent need to repent and believe before their time runs out.

Perhaps your illness is not terminal, but you live with chronic pain. You live with a daily, throbbing reminder that all is not as it should be. This is a message that our control-happy, fix-it culture desperately needs to hear. There are some problems that can't be solved by joining a gym or making more money or finding people who understand you. Our world is broken, and all the brainpower or buying power that exists cannot mend it. If your pain increases your longing for heaven, and you speak up about that hope, you will be a powerful sign pointing to the restoration that will come when Christ returns.

There are many other categories of illness, and the purpose or the parable of your illness may not be immediately obvious to you. Your illness may be messy. It may be someone else's fault.

It may be hard to untangle from your own sinful, addictive behaviors. But I assure you that it is not beyond God's power to tell his story through you. It is only by digging deeply into God's story that we can hope to understand our own.

Strength Made Perfect in Weakness

There's another way that you can allow God's glory to shine through your story, and that's by allowing his strength to be made perfect in your weakness. On the one-year anniversary of Tim's death, Annie asked friends to write to her and tell her how we had seen God redeeming Tim's cancer. I wrote:

> Since knowing Tim and watching him suffer from cancer, I no longer have any trouble understanding these words from 2 Corinthians 12:9, "My grace is sufficient for you, for my power is made perfect in weakness." Tim was, at the same time, the weakest person I knew and the strongest person I knew. The weaker his body got, the more it was clear that his stamina was not from his ranger training, his healthy lifestyle, or even his character. It was the Holy Spirit, sustaining Tim. I think of the image of an oil lamp. The wick should burn up, but it doesn't as long as it continues to draw from the oil. Tim would have given up years ago if he was running the race in his own strength, but God's strength sustained him to the end. If Tim hadn't endured the weakness, we would not have seen the strength. If Tim had lived a long, healthy life and died a pain-free death, we would all still have said what a great, strong, competent person Tim was, but we would never have seen so vividly the power of God manifest in his willing servant.

As long as you feel strong, you and everyone around you may be tempted to believe that you *are* strong. When you know, beyond a shadow of a doubt, that you are weak, you become a vessel for God's strength to be manifest in you. Are you willing for God to shine through you in this way?

Polly Carey was the daughter of a weaver in Northampton-shire, England. We wouldn't know of her if she hadn't been the sister of William Carey, the man we call the "Father of Modern Missions." Polly was afflicted with a degenerative disease of the spine. While her brother spent his life as a missionary to India, Polly spent hers in dependence upon other people. By the time she was twenty-five years old, she was completely paralyzed except for the use of her right arm. She lived with her sister Ann and was confined to her bed for over fifty years. For the last three decades of her life, she was unable to speak and communicated by writing on a slate.

Polly didn't choose this life for herself. At times her discontentment showed through in her correspondence. Yet in spite of the fact that her ministry was not conspicuous, she had a powerful effect on the nation of India—and the modern missionary movement—through her prayers for her brother and the encouragement she gave him through her letters to the end of his life. She nurtured the women in her village by teaching a Bible class, even though her pupils had to crowd around her bed!

Polly's chronic illness made her dependent on her brother for financial support and her sister for her physical care. More importantly, it made her dependent on the Holy Spirit for her joy, significance, and influence. Her pastor is reported to have said of her, "Her work in her affliction, in its way, was as great as that which her great brother wrought."[7]

We naturally assume that if God is going to use us, it will be through an active life characterized by fulfilling work and ministry and a busy family life. But God may choose a different path that is equally necessary for his kingdom and shows his power through our powerlessness.

As you wait, keep praying for healing, but pray also for God's strength to be perfected in your weakness as long as he withholds health. There is no body so broken that it cannot be offered to God as a living sacrifice, and there is no arm too feeble to wield the sword of the Spirit.

5

Waiting for a Home

The Kingdom of God is where we belong. It is home, and whether we realize it or not, I think we are all of us homesick for it.

Frederick Buechner, Secrets in the Dark

Chris and Mandy each grew up on the mission field. Mandy's missionary parents worked in Kazakhstan, while Chris grew up with his family in the Solomon Islands in the South Pacific. They met at boarding school, and they shared a desire to return to the mission field.

I met them when Chris came to seminary in Alabama. By then they had two children. Chris and Mandy planned to move to the Solomon Islands where he would minister as a pastor and Bible translator. As his seminary graduation neared, church leaders from the Solomon Islands asked Chris to get a PhD before moving back to the islands so that he could train other pastors at the seminary level.

Chris was accepted into a PhD program in New Zealand, so they moved their family (which now included a third child) across the world. Each child was allowed to bring a couple of favorite toys, but they sold or gave away the vast majority of their belongings, taking with them only what could fit in their suitcases.

While in New Zealand, Mandy gave birth to a fourth child. Chris finished his doctorate in record time, and they moved around the world once again. By this time the older children had grown accustomed to life down under and didn't want to leave. Yet they once again had to choose a favorite toy and pack their suitcases.

To raise financial support, Chris and Mandy traveled around the US for over a year, staying in the homes of friends and family. Finally, after raising enough money and securing the correct visas, they moved to the Pacific. They reached their ministry goal, but their children will forever be "third culture" kids who won't feel entirely at home in any one culture.

While Chris and Mandy are living a life of faithfulness to God's calling, they have had to sacrifice the comforts of putting down roots or nesting or making friends who will travel with them through life. They are a living picture of Hebrews 13:14: "For here we have no lasting city, but we seek the city that is to come."

Homesick in Our Homes

G. K. Chesterton said that "men are homesick in their homes."[8] While most of us have more than adequate shelter, many of us still live with unfulfilled longings for home. You may long for home because you have moved around so much that you don't really know where home is. You may live far away from your family and long to live near them. You may long for family you would want to live near. Some people live with a longing for a home in which they feel safe and loved.

My friend Stacy lived in foster care from the time she was twelve until she was eighteen. She had five different foster homes in six years, and she was moved around through group homes and detention centers while waiting on placement over twenty different times. Without roots or stability, she felt very unwanted. She learned not to get attached to anyone because she never knew when she would next be moved. She still struggles to feel secure even now that she's an adult.

Sometimes life can feel like one long transition. I heard one single woman describe her longing for home as the desire to live somewhere for ten years. She lived from year to year with different roommates in different places. She longed for a home she could nest in, knowing she wouldn't have to pack up when the year's lease ran out. Her longing wasn't really for a house, but for permanence and roots.

Maybe you've had a home but have it no longer. Maybe the loss of a spouse has forced you to give up the home you created together. If your parents have passed away, you may have had the experience of selling the home of your childhood memories. You and your siblings have divided up the china from which you ate holiday meals and donated your mother's and grandmother's cookware to someone in need. Breaking up a home after someone dies is a necessary life passage, but from an earthly perspective, it is terribly sad.

Why are we homesick? Even though our longings for home may focus on what is less than ideal about where we live or whom we live with, deep down we are homesick because *this is not our home*. If you are a believer in Jesus, you are a citizen of heaven (Phil. 3:20). We live on earth, but "we are waiting for new heavens and a new earth in which righteousness dwells" (2 Pet. 3:13).

Living as Sojourners

From the beginning of God's dealings with his people, he has promised them a home. Paradoxically, God's promise to Abraham to give him his own land and make him into a great nation hinged on Abraham leaving his home in the land of Ur (Genesis 12). When he left Ur, he left behind the gods that his fathers worshiped. Abraham obeyed God, but the land that God promised him was full of other nations who worshiped other gods. The writer of Hebrews summarizes Abraham's life this way:

> By faith Abraham obeyed when he was called to go out to a place that he was to receive as an inheritance. And he went out, not knowing where he was going. By faith he went to live in the land of promise, as in a foreign land, living in tents with Isaac and Jacob, heirs with him of the same promise. (Heb. 11:8–9)

Abraham lived in the Promised Land, but he lived there as a sojourner. He didn't farm the land or build a palace for himself. He lived in tents and grazed sheep. The father of God's chosen people, the one who had been promised a land for his promised descendants, was a nomad. But Abraham did not consider God's promise to have failed. He looked ahead for something greater: "For he was looking forward to the city that has foundations, whose designer and builder is God" (Heb. 11:10).

Abraham believed God's promise that there would be a day when his descendants would own the land God had pledged to him and would not have to live there as strangers among nations serving other gods. This promise was temporarily fulfilled during the reigns of David and Solomon. But it will be perfectly and permanently fulfilled when the spiritual sons of Abraham dwell in the New Jerusalem (Rev. 21:9–27). When Abraham died, the only piece of land he owned was the cave he was buried in, which he bought from the Hittites. Hebrews says of him and his sons,

> These all died in faith, not having received the things promised, but having seen them and greeted them from afar, and having acknowledged that they were strangers and exiles on the earth. For people who speak thus make it clear that they are seeking a homeland. If they had been thinking of that land from which they had gone out, they would have had opportunity to return. But as it is, they desire a better country, that is, a heavenly one. Therefore God is not ashamed to be called their God, for he has prepared for them a city. (Heb. 11:13–16).

Abraham did not return to the land of his fathers or to the gods they worshiped. He preferred to live in tents for the present knowing that a heavenly city awaited him. He knew it would be a home worth waiting for.

Living as Exiles

Exiles live differently than immigrants. An immigrant has chosen a new homeland. He and his family assimilate. They learn the language and customs, and he never expects his children to return to the land they have left. But to call someone an exile implies that he would prefer to be in his homeland. He had to leave, but he hopes to return. Whether he is living in a refugee camp or an embassy, he strives to keep his national identity intact.

The prophet Daniel was truly an exile in Babylon. Brought from his homeland of Judah by the order of King Nebuchadnezzar, he was thrust into the lavish life of a Babylonian palace. Daniel knew that he couldn't eat the rich food and wine he would be served (which had probably been offered as sacrifices to pagan gods) if he was to keep the Law of Moses that God had graciously given to the Jewish people. Daniel chose to keep the law of the God of Israel even though he was in a place where it would have been to his advantage to assimilate and worship the local gods.

Daniel didn't make himself a nuisance to the Babylonians. In fact, he was so wise that he became invaluable to the rulers of the empire, first Nebuchadnezzar, and then Darius after him. Living as a faithful exile earned Daniel enemies as well. He found such favor with the king that other officials were jealous and sought to do away with him. They said, "We shall not find any ground for complaint against this Daniel unless we find it in connection with the law of his God" (Dan. 6:5).

Daniel's enemies decided to exploit his faithfulness. When they passed a law that no one could pray to any god but King Darius, Daniel chose to obey God's law rather than man's. He kept on praying to the God of Israel three times a day, just like his enemies knew he would, and he landed in a lions' den. King Darius was so distraught over losing his trusted counselor that he stayed up all night waiting to see how Daniel fared. When he found him alive the next morning, he praised Daniel's God and threw Daniel's accusers into the lions' den.

What was Daniel praying for three times a day? He was praying that God would return his people to the Promised Land. Yet even as he pined and prayed, he served others in his exile. He lived like a Jew rather than a Babylonian or a Persian, and he did not compromise his identity as a child of the promise. If you feel like an exile, out of step with aspects of the culture of this world and sometimes despised, you are in good company.

The Promise of Home

Christians in every age have left their homes for the sake of spreading the gospel. They can do this, trusting Jesus's promise to restore what has been sacrificed: "And everyone who has left houses or brothers or sisters or father or mother or children or lands, for my name's sake, will receive a hundredfold and will inherit eternal life" (Matt. 19:29).

Jesus does not ask us to give what he himself withheld. He left his home with his Father to come to earth to redeem us. Although he had an earthly family, he spent the three years of his ministry traveling around, dependent on others for their hospitality. He warned those who would follow him, "Foxes have holes, and birds of the air have nests, but the Son of Man has nowhere to lay his head" (Luke 9:58).

Those who leave their homes for the sake of Christ don't do it because their ties to home are weak. Instead, their ties to their heavenly home, the one Jesus promises, are so much stronger that they are freed to let go of earthly houses, family roots, and worldly goods.

I had some friends who bought a house that needed extensive renovation. While they waited for the work to be completed, they lived in an apartment. They didn't spend their months in the apartment complaining about how small and inadequate it was for their family. They knew they would soon move into their dream house. The knowledge of the home that awaited them made the months they spent in cramped quarters easy to endure. They are a parable of how we should wait. Fixing our eyes on the home that is to come will help us thrive in this world that is not our home.

Waiting Well While Waiting for a Home

Does the fact that we are not yet in our eternal home mean that we shouldn't care where or how we live? Does it mean that you should stop recycling and resign from your neighborhood association? Not at all. C. S. Lewis presents a very different picture of the sojourner's mind-set:

> If you read history you will find that the Christians who did most for the present world were just those who thought most of the next. The Apostles themselves, who set on foot the conversion of the Roman Empire, the great men who built up the Middle Ages, the English Evangelicals who abolished the Slave Trade, all left their mark on Earth, precisely because their minds were occupied with Heaven. It is since Christians have largely ceased to think of the other world that they have become so ineffective in this. Aim at Heaven and you will get earth "thrown in": aim at earth and you will get neither.[9]

What Lewis gets at is the truth of Jesus's words in Matthew 16:25: "For whoever would save his life will lose it, but whoever loses his life for my sake will find it." When you know your home is in heaven, you are willing to take more risks in this life. You can make sacrifices on behalf of your neighbor because you're not obsessed with protecting what is yours.

Waiting for your heavenly home should free you to invite all kinds of people into your earthly home. You can welcome the poor and the little child without being afraid they will take something or break something. But rather than making you careless and neglectful of your home, a heavenly mind-set should inspire you to make your home welcoming and pleasant for others.

I've noticed that the people who tend to be best at welcoming friends and acquaintances into their homes for holidays are those who live in a place where they don't have extended family. If you live in the city where you grew up and are surrounded by relatives, you probably have family obligations around holidays. If your family eats Christmas Eve dinner at your grandmother's house and Christmas brunch at your in-laws', you may not have the freedom to invite along those from your church who don't have Christmas plans. Yet people who live far from their hometown and family have the opportunity to welcome strangers into their homes on these special days. There's more room at the table.

Expat communities overseas are great at banding together to celebrate the holidays of their home countries. Americans living everywhere from Scotland to Singapore celebrate Thanksgiving with the closest thing to a turkey they can find. This should be our model as we seek to live as citizens of heaven at home on this earth. We are joined to other Christians by a love for our homeland. We can celebrate in the fellowship of that common citizenship any time two believers are together, not just at holidays. And like expats who welcome locals into their homes to teach them about their homeland's traditions, we should be eager to bring the lost to our table. The more the merrier.

A House with Many Rooms

In the course of writing this book, the need to wait in hope for my heavenly home has become very personal to me. I left my hometown where I had deep roots and strong ties to move to New York City where my husband is following God's call on his life. I left a place where real estate is affordable and kids grow up with backyards to come to a city where population density and exorbitant rent mean we must live in just a few rooms. I had to severely cull my earthly possessions down to what will fit in the limited closet space in our "cozy" apartment. As I felt tempted to grieve for the home I was leaving and the possessions I was dispersing, I kept reminding myself that although the next step for me was a tiny apartment, my ultimate destination is a house with many rooms.

You might think that a truly spiritual person wouldn't long for a big house with lots of rooms. But that's exactly what Jesus promises us:

> Let not your hearts be troubled. Believe in God; believe also in me. In my Father's house are many rooms. If it were not so, would I have told you that I go to prepare a place for you? And if I go to prepare a place for you, I will come again and will take you to myself, that where I am you may be also. (John 14:1–3)

This house is not only large, it is well-prepared. In my mind, that conjures up images of fresh paint, a stocked pantry, and new linens. And while you may never live in a house big enough to hold all of the people you love, this one will. Not only will there be a place for us, there will be rooms for all of those that you love who have been born again to eternal life. But it won't be the many rooms or the other people in them that will make this house our home.

I once had a roommate that fell in love with a man she met in Europe. She lived in Georgia, so their courtship was transatlantic. As she fell deeper and deeper in love with him, her all-consuming desire was to be with him. I'm pretty sure she would have lived in a one-room shack with no plumbing if he was there. Home for her was more about the person she wanted to be with than a place or creature comforts.

We will only truly be at home when we are with our Bridegroom. While the visions of heaven described in the book of Revelation include bejeweled gates and golden streets, these are not the main attraction. Heaven will be heaven because God will be there. We probably won't even notice the sea of glass or the pearl gates because our eyes will be for our beloved. To be with him will be to be at home at last.

6

Waiting for a Prodigal

Does that lamp still burn in my Father's house,
Which he kindled the night I went away?

Christina Rossetti, "A Prodigal Son"

prod•i•gal (adj.) recklessly extravagant; wayward

Susan remembers her firstborn son Martin as a delightful little boy. He was tenderhearted and funny, and he loved his little sister. When Martin was nine, his dad left. While Susan knows this deeply wounded her son, he never talked about it much or acknowledged it bothered him.

Martin continued to be a good kid and a good student into his teen years. He went off to college and was accepted to law school. Susan noticed he seemed to be struggling a bit in his senior year of college, but she told herself not to worry.

During Martin's first semester of graduate school, his life started to fall apart. Susan found marijuana in his room. While the discovery was devastating, she told herself, "Now I've caught him, and he'll quit." Martin didn't quit, and he had to drop out of graduate school. He spiraled down as drug addiction gripped him and became the driving force of his life.

Susan was devastated. She couldn't understand why this was happening to her precious son. She questioned why other parents' children turned out fine. This wasn't supposed to happen to her family! The pain of watching her son destroy himself consumed her. She thought about him all the time.

As Martin continued on for years in the throes of addiction, Susan cycled through different phases of grief and emotion. At times she would distance herself from him. She'd back off and try not to think about it or find out what was happening with him. She would bury her pain.

After a while, Susan's sympathy and compassion would come flooding back and break down the walls she built between her and her pain. She would try to help Martin who, in spite of his bondage to drugs, was still as tenderhearted and funny as he had always been. He went through rehab and relapses several times. There were times when he was homeless, and there were many times when Susan had no idea where he was.

Susan brought her heart, broken by grief over her son, to the Lord. For years she wrestled with God, asking him why he had allowed this to happen to *her* son. One day when she was praying, she finally understood the answer to her question. Martin's life of addiction was no surprise to God, and he had sovereignly chosen Susan to be his mother.

This realization reoriented Susan's thinking. It allowed her to see Martin not as a problem to be solved but as someone God had entrusted to her to love no matter what.

Susan considered this the final stage of acceptance of her

son's drug addiction and her calling to love him. She once heard someone say that God has trouble with his children too, and this thought comforts her. Martin's story isn't over, and Susan continues to hope and pray that he won't always be a prodigal. She still struggles, but she says confidently, "Whatever the future holds, he's my son, and I wouldn't trade him for anybody."

The Prodigal Son

It's not hard to understand how a parent's love for a prodigal child can be a kingdom parable because that's the point of the most famous parable Jesus ever told. In Luke 15, Jesus tells the story of a wealthy man with two sons. One requests his inheritance early, leaves home, and lives like there's no tomorrow. His profligate lifestyle comes to an end when he runs out of money and hits rock bottom. He hires himself out to a pig farmer, but he's so hungry even the pigs' food looks good to him.

When he comes to his senses, he realizes that if he's going to be a servant, he might as well be a servant in his father's house where the hired hands are well fed. We don't know whether he has repented or regrets the pain he's given to his father. But we do know that his father embraced him before he could get a word out of his mouth. He isn't made a servant, but instead he's celebrated as if he were a returning war hero. The father wants all around him to share his joy, proclaiming, "For this my son was dead, and is alive again; he was lost, and is found" (Luke 15:24).

Jesus told this parable, along with the stories of the lost sheep and the lost coin, in response to Pharisees who chided him for eating with sinners. The father in the story didn't care that his son had nothing to show for his inheritance or that he had been hanging around with (unclean) swine. He had his son back. Jesus ate with sinners because they are the prodigal sons and daughters of God. They don't deserve a place at the table, but God offers them one because he loves them. We don't deserve a place at the table, but he gives us one because he loves us. He's our Father.

The Prodigal Spouse

There's another parable of a prodigal in the Bible. It isn't told by Jesus; instead it was lived in real life by the prophet Hosea. God told Hosea to marry a prostitute. He took her away from the men who had bought her, gave her a home, and had children by her. She didn't stay with him, but instead ran away to her old life, the life he had rescued her from.

God wouldn't let Hosea let his wife go. He directed him to go and buy her back. Only think of how painful it must have been for a husband whose wife has run away from his loving provision to have to purchase her from another man. But Hosea did it because God has done that for us. Though she had not loved him, he loved her.

Through Hosea's story, God sent a powerful message to his people. Though they had served other gods and run away from his love, he wasn't through with them. He loved them and would redeem them so they could come back into the safety of his love. He said, "I will heal their apostasy; I will love them freely, for my anger has turned from them" (Hos. 14:4).

Tragically, husbands and wives still live out this painful parable today. Lynn and her husband had been married for twelve years when she started to realize that there was something really wrong with her marriage. She didn't suspect an affair at first because she couldn't believe that her husband, a professing Christian, would violate his marriage vows. He was a doctor and often worked late, but one Christmas Eve, he didn't come home at all.

That Christmas was the start of years of unfaithfulness, separations, and attempts at reconciliation. Lynn's husband would lie about his affairs, making it nearly impossible to tell when, if ever, his repentance was genuine. Lynn vividly remembers sitting with him at a coffee shop where he asked her to forgive him for his infidelity, yet all the while she knew that his plan after leaving the coffee shop was to go and sleep with another woman.

Lynn prayed for her husband to repent. They went through hundreds of hours of counseling sessions together. She could have divorced him early on, but her heart's desire was for their relationship to be restored and their family made whole. She didn't just want him to stop having affairs and start living an upright life. She longed to know his heart, but he didn't want to be known. Instead, he betrayed her again and again.

If you have been forsaken by your spouse or your spouse has forsaken God, like Lynn, you know something of the pain Hosea experienced. And you know something of the pain God experiences each time one of his children forsakes his steadfast love for some fleeting pleasure the world can offer. He isn't just looking for good behavior; he's looking for intimacy with us.

Satan, the Multitasker

When Satan goes after our family, he also goes after us. He loves to kill two birds with one stone. When your child or your spouse is caught up in sin or unbelief, it is highly tempting to make that person the center of your faith. Your spiritual walk can become not about your salvation through faith in Christ, but a desperate campaign to save the prodigal you love. As time goes on, if you don't see an answer to your prayers for your prodigal, you may be tempted to doubt.

Conversely, you may be tempted to harden your heart as did the elder brother in the parable of the prodigal. Even as you pray for your prodigal to repent, you may find yourself comparing your own life path with his and feeling pretty pleased with yourself. You may find yourself thinking, "I would never do what he has done," even though you might not say it out loud. Beware self-righteousness. It is just as destructive to the soul as promiscuity, and far more deceptive.

When Satan attacks someone you love, he attempts to attack your faith at the same time, either by doubt or by pride. You don't have to fall victim to his scheme. By God's grace, waiting on a prodigal can actually strengthen your faith. One woman whose husband forsook Christ midway through their marriage told me that the sad events had enabled her to reach a turning point in her faith. She realized that even her husband's crisis of faith was something God could use for her good. God wanted her faith to grow in spite of her husband's loss of faith. She couldn't just tread water while she waited for her husband to return. She grew and flourished, becoming even more dependent on God after her husband was no longer walking with her spiritually.

Lynn had a similar turning point when she started attending a church that emphasized the sovereignty of God. "I remember many times thinking, if God wanted things to be different in our marriage, he could change it in a heartbeat. But he wasn't choosing to do that." Rather than making her bitter toward God, this recognition brought her comfort. It helped her realize that even her husband's unfaithfulness was something God could use for good in her life.

The very best thing you could do for the prodigal in your life is to grow in your own faith. He or she needs you to be a prayer warrior, and warriors need good nourishment. If you pursue God with all your heart, soul, and strength while you wait on your prodigal's return, one of Satan's favorite strategies will be thwarted.

Another way that Satan may try to multitask is to destroy other relationships in your life. If you have a prodigal child, you and your husband may find yourselves at odds over how to interact with him or her. One of you may be ready to practice tough love while the other may want to come to the rescue. Couples must resist the temptation to turn against each other while waiting on a prodigal. Even if you disagree on how to approach your prodigal, do everything in your power to keep your child's sin from destroying your marriage.

The Bible calls Satan "the Accuser." When your child runs from God, the Enemy will try to weigh you down with guilt. "It's your fault," he will say. "You deserve this." If you are conscious of sinful failings as a parent, confess these to God. Then accept that Jesus has already paid the penalty for them. If you keep pulling your old sins out of the drawer, you effectively say Christ's death isn't enough to cover your sin. The same is true if you keep recalling your spouse's sin. There is no parenting failure beyond God's forgiveness.

If you've been abandoned by your spouse, the Accuser will attack your self-worth. He may tell you that you weren't pretty enough or smart enough. He will remind you of all the ways you didn't measure up. You must fight this by finding your worth in your identity as a redeemed child of God. You were so precious to God that Jesus died for you. He didn't do this because you were pretty or smart or had your act together; he did it because he wanted you to be his.

Waiting Well While Waiting for a Prodigal

Prayer is a huge part of waiting on prodigals. We pray that they will return and repent. We pray that God will restore broken relationships and redeem the years that have been squandered. We pray, to paraphrase Augustine's words, that their hearts would stay restless until they finally rest in God.[10]

People who are waiting for a prodigal go through different cycles of grief and acceptance, just as Susan did. It is good to recognize this. While one week you may be full of hope, the next you may feel angry. There may be times when you feel weary of the prodigal. Stay honest before the Lord, and pray according to where you are emotionally, not according to where you think you should be.

One mother of a prodigal told me about a season when it was very hard for her to pray. She knew that Luke 18:1 said that we "ought always to pray and not lose heart." But she was so brokenhearted over her son and had prayed so long for his salvation that she felt as if she had run out of prayers. The only thing she could find to say to God was the verse reference "Luke 18:1." She prayed this all day, every day, knowing that God knew her heart and desire for her son's repentance and that he would accept a simple verse reference as her prayer.

You may feel shame over your prodigal, but I encourage you not to hide your situation from others. God is glorified when he answers prayer, and if others are praying for the prodigal in your life, God's glory will be magnified if your prodigal returns. You may worry that others will judge you as a parent or a spouse, but is fear of that judgment worth cutting yourself off from the prayers of the body of Christ, prayers that could move your prodigal to repentance?

Perhaps you are a leader in your church, and you fear that people will think you are a fraud if they discover that your child has rebelled or your marriage has fallen apart. While it may be true that people will see you differently once they discover your family isn't perfect, you will likely be surprised at new doors of ministry that will open. No one wants to unburden herself to someone who has never suffered. When you go public with your pain, you will find that others will be eager to share their own fears and failings with you.

Look for ways that God has used your painful situation to draw you closer to him. For years, Lynn feared that if she lost her marriage, she would lose her identity. But as her husband continued in unrepentance and she clung to God's promises, her identity in Christ took on greater importance than her identity as a wife. She recalls, "God really began to show me more of who he is and who I am, apart from being attached to somebody else." You don't have to wait to find out how your prodigal's story turns out to celebrate God's ongoing work in your own life, just as he worked in Lynn's.

As you wait for your prodigal, I hope that you will cling to God's promises. During her years of waiting, Lynn carried around a little ringed notebook with Scripture passages to meditate on when her fears overwhelmed her. She clung to Isaiah 41:10, which she memorized in the New American Standard version:

> Do not fear, for I am with you;
> Do not anxiously look about you, for I am your God.
> I will strengthen you, surely I will help you,
> Surely I will uphold you with My righteous right hand.

In a sense, Lynn's fears came true in that she and her husband did eventually divorce after thirty-five years of marriage. But her fears of being alone and without financial provision fell away as God kept his promises and the body of Christ supported her. While she still wouldn't choose her story to unfold the way it did, she says of her loss, "I know God has used it mightily in my life for his purposes." God's promises never fail.

A Parable of God's Love

The pain over the broken relationship with the prodigal in your life will give you a glimpse into the sorrow God feels when we run from him. The lengths to which you would go to restore your prodigal reflects the perseverance of the Good Shepherd who goes out in search of his sheep. By watching and waiting for your prodigal's return, you are living a parable of God's undeserved love for us.

But while your grief is a powerful picture of God's grief over the lost, your love, as strong as it may be, is an imperfect reflection of his. As sinful human beings, our love is too often laced with pride and selfishness. Maybe you are furious at your prodigal for destroying your reputation. Maybe there are times when you want him to suffer for what he's done to you.

If you find yourself responding sinfully to your prodigal, let that sin send you running to your Father. Even as you live the role of the parent or spouse of a prodigal, we must remember that in relation to God, we are all prodigal sons and daughters. He is just as willing to forgive you for imperfectly loving your prodigal as the father was to forgive his son for squandering his inheritance.

Nothing better illustrates God's grace than his love for prodigals. They don't work their way back into his favor. He doesn't wait for them to clean up before he lets them into his presence; he washes their feet and gives them clean clothes to wear.

If you love a prodigal, you are a living embodiment of God's love for the lost. The prodigal may have done everything possible to destroy your trust and good will, but you love him anyway. You don't love him because he deserves it, but because he is yours. And that is how God loves you.

7

Sustained While We Wait

In every condition, in sickness, in health;
In poverty's vale, or abounding in wealth;
At home and abroad, on the land, on the sea,
As thy days may demand, shall thy strength ever be.

"How Firm a Foundation"

In this book, I've made the case that waiting has theological significance. God intends our waiting seasons to tell the story of his people waiting on his return to take us to our eternal home. I hope you are getting excited about that.

The question remains, how can we wait well for a lifetime? If our waiting may not end in this life, how do we press on until the end? Maybe singleness is not so bad today, but can you bear it for the rest of your life? Maybe you have peace in the face of your cancer diagnosis, but where will you get the strength to cope with seemingly endless cycles of chemotherapy?

If you feel like you don't have the fortitude for a lifetime of waiting, that's because God doesn't give grace in a lifetime supply. He provides it one day at a time. If you doubt that God has given you the capacity to endure your trial for a lifetime, you can rest assured that he hasn't. But he has given you exactly what you need to flourish today.

Jesus sought daily strength from his Father (Mark 1:35; Luke 5:15–16). He expected God to provide what he needed day by day (Luke 11:3). God promises us the same timely help in Christ:

> For we do not have a high priest who is unable to sympathize with our weaknesses, but one who in every respect has been tempted as we are, yet without sin. Let us then with confidence draw near to the throne of grace, that we may receive mercy and find *grace to help in time of need.* (Heb. 4:15–16)

God has promised to supply what we need, when we need it. He hasn't equipped us for hypotheticals. As C. S. Lewis wrote in a letter to Mary Willis Shelburne, "It is seldom the present & the actual that is intolerable. Remember one is given the strength to bear what happens to one, but not the 100 and 1 different things that might happen."[11]

You Can't Buy Manna in Bulk

It's a great feeling when you can stock up on food and paper products at a wholesale store and know you won't have to go back for months. But God doesn't allow us to stock up on his grace. He gives it to us one day at a time.

One of my favorite Bible stories is God's provision of bread in the wilderness. The Israelites grumbled because they had no food, so God gave them manna from heaven. The flaky food would appear on the ground in the morning. They could gather as much as they liked, but it didn't do any good to store it up. With the exception of the Sabbath eve (when they were allowed to gather the next day's portion), if they kept manna overnight, it became full of worms with a terrible smell. I'm sure they didn't make that mistake more than a couple of times.

It may have taken a while for the children of Israel to trust that the manna would be there the next morning. They had to adjust to going to bed with full stomachs but empty cupboards. You might have thought that after a while, God would have started feeding them some other way, but Exodus 16:35 says, "The people of Israel ate the manna forty years, till they came to a habitable land. They ate the manna till they came to the border of the land of Canaan."

You see, once you start walking in daily dependence on God, you have to *keep* walking in it. God's desire is to be in fellowship with us, and one way he draws us into that fellowship is by meeting our needs one day at a time. He doesn't just give us what we need; he wants to give us himself. He gives us himself through his Word. The trials of our life that make us crave the life-giving sustenance of the daily nourishment of Scripture are like the hunger pains that drive us to the daily food our bodies need to survive.

In the first chapter of this book, I argued that God isn't preparing us to graduate from the School of Waiting. We should want to learn how to wait well so that we can go on waiting well because we will always be waiting for something in this life. The Israelites lived on manna for forty years, and if your particular season of waiting lasts for forty years, God will supply your daily needs.

If you are walking through infertility, my question for you is, can you live for the next twenty-four hours without a child?

Can you trust God to get you through today? If the answer is yes, then you have what it takes to survive for the long haul. You just need to ask yourself the same question tomorrow. The same thing is true of every other season of waiting described in this book.

Bread and Fish All Around

Centuries after God provided manna in the desert, he spread another table in the wilderness for a large group of hungry people. A crowd of thousands had gathered to hear Jesus, and there wasn't food anywhere for them to eat. This wasn't a conference center or fairground full of food trucks. His disciples realized they had a problem on their hands. But Jesus didn't see any problem because he was there. He took two fish and five barley loaves and fed the entire crowd as much as they wanted.

Sometimes when we look at our circumstances, we realize there are going to be problems meeting our needs. Maybe you need companionship as a single woman, but your friends keep getting married or moving away. Maybe you want to adopt a child, but you're living paycheck to paycheck. Maybe you're sick and need someone to take care of you, but you feel like you've exhausted all of your friends already. God does not look at your situation and wring his hands. He is not limited by the resources you have at your disposal.

The first step toward allowing God to meet your needs is to pray that he will. As obvious as that sounds, it's amazing how often we fail to take that step. If I can't imagine how God could meet a need, I won't bring it before him. I foolishly assume that I need to figure out *how* he might answer a request in order to ask it. But God delights when we give him unsolvable puzzles, and he explicitly tells us that he can do "far more abundantly than all we ask or think" (Eph. 3:20).

You can bring him your bread and fish, or lack thereof, and ask him to feed a crowd of thousands. You can look at your future without a clue how God will meet your needs over the course of a lifetime and trust that he will. But you have to wait for him to reveal his provision day by day.

Seeing Jesus Is Not a Consolation Prize

I once went on a retreat during a time when I felt especially sad about my singleness. The speaker spoke about the story from Luke 2 of Anna the prophetess. In her youth, Anna had been married for seven years before her husband died leaving her a widow. At eighty-four years old, she spent all her time, day and night, praying in the temple. We don't know whether she had any children, but at the point when we meet her in Luke, she was alone.

The speaker showed us a painting. In the picture, Mary held her baby next to the prophet Simeon in the foreground. Anna was behind them looking on. As I looked at the painting, I felt rebellion rise in me. I wrote in my journal, "Anna's lot has been given to me: to wait alone upon the Lord. I do not want to be Anna. I want to be Mary with the child in her arms."

Even as I confessed my dissatisfaction with my life, I knew my perspective was off. Anna had not been given a consolation prize. She had lived her life waiting and hoping for the Messiah, and God had allowed her to see him. This solitary octogenarian had lived to see her salvation.

We would never choose suffering for ourselves. But when God allows suffering into our lives, he gives us opportunities to experience Jesus that we would not otherwise have. If Anna had been home surrounded by children and grandchildren, she would not have been in the temple that day, and she wouldn't have met the hope of Israel. While you may not literally lay eyes on Jesus as she did, God wants to give you a richer, deeper experience of himself that is more precious than the thing he has withheld from you. God won't waste your waiting.

How do I know that? The Bible is full of promises that those who wait for God will be rewarded:

> Therefore the LORD waits to be gracious to you,
>   and therefore he exalts himself to show mercy to you.
> For the LORD is a God of justice;
>   blessed are all those who wait for him. (Isa. 30:18)

> Indeed, none who wait for you shall be put to shame.
>   (Ps. 25:3a)

> From of old no one has heard
>   or perceived by the ear,
>   no eye has seen a God besides you,
>   who acts for those who wait for him. (Isa. 64:4)

> They who wait for the LORD shall renew their strength.
>   (Isa. 40:31a)

These are just a few of many. If we choose to wait not just on our problems to go away but to wait upon the Lord, we can expect God to bless that waiting.

When Vaneetha Rendall recalls the trials in her life, the list is staggering: As a child, she contracted polio and underwent numerous surgeries and yearlong hospital stays. She was bullied and teased by classmates. After she grew up and married, she suffered multiple miscarriages, followed by the death of her infant son due to a doctor's mistake. Then, debilitating pain and diminished use of her limbs led to a diagnosis of post-polio syndrome. Finally, her husband left her and her two daughters. She says, "Losing my child, my health, and my marriage almost made me lose my mind."

Reflecting on a life full of pain, Rendall writes, "If it were up to me, I would have written my story differently. . . . Each line represents something hard. Gut wrenching. Life changing. But now, in retrospect, I wouldn't erase a single line."[12]

How can Rendall say this? Because, she writes, "In the midst of my deepest pain, in the darkness, God's presence has been unmistakable." She does not view God's nearness as a consolation prize.

Anna waited in the temple each day without knowing whether she would live to see the Messiah. After seeing Jesus, she could have wholeheartedly affirmed Psalm 84:10, which says, "a day in your courts is better than a thousand elsewhere." Maybe you can't say that wholeheartedly now. But on the other side of our waiting, I've no doubt that we will count knowing God as more valuable than any of his blessings we had to wait for.

Crying Out to God

In your waiting, you may reach a place where you have no words left to pray. You may be in so much pain that you feel like you cannot put it into words.

I want you to know that prayer does not have to be formed into words for God to understand us. If all you can do is cry to God, he is trustworthy to receive it. He knows how to listen out for a cry. In Psalm 34:15, David writes, "The eyes of the LORD are toward the righteous and his ears toward their cry." He goes on to say, "When the righteous cry for help, the LORD hears and delivers them out of all their troubles" (v. 17). These verses do not say God is attentive only to prayers that have sound theology or that last at least twenty minutes or that even follow a biblical pattern. God hears even a cry.

Think about crying as communication. In the course of an infant's life, his first real means of articulation is his cry. Although babies in the womb remind their mothers of their presence by kicks and somersaults, the cry is the first communication the child makes with the world. It carries a very simple message: something is wrong.

The infant plays the easy part in the exchange; he merely sounds the warning. It is the parents' responsibility to determine the source of his discomfort and seek a remedy. I doubt that the infant even understands the need behind the cry; otherwise, why wouldn't a baby who is overtired just go to sleep instead of crying? No, the infant only senses that crying is the appropriate way to express his bewildering need to someone who can do something about it. In this sense, the cry is the articulation of the inarticulate.

A cry does not express an end goal. It merely expresses a need. Women sometimes take a bad rap when they cry without knowing the reason. But crying is particularly appropriate when you can't put your needs or frustrations into words. It expresses that we need help, though we may not be sure what kind of help we need.

God is not looking for us to express our need of him articulately before he will draw near to us to help us. God does not save us on the basis of our self-awareness or our insight; he lifts up those who are crushed in spirit (Ps. 34:18). When the most that we can do is cry, that is enough. It puts us into the receiving position of a little child, which is one of the marks of those who will enter God's kingdom (Mark 10:15).

We can follow the example of the psalmist by directing our cries to God. We can even adopt the words of the psalmist and other parts of Scripture as our prayers. Although we may not know what we need or how it can be accomplished, like an infant we know who can meet the need. Romans 8:26 assures us, "Likewise the Spirit helps us in our weakness. For we do not know what to pray for as we ought, but the Spirit himself intercedes for us with groanings too deep for words."

Loving Your Neighbor

While we are waiting, what should we do with ourselves? We can turn for direction to Jesus's summary of all of God's commandments. "You shall love the Lord your God with all your heart and with all your soul and with all your mind. This is the great and first commandment. And a second is like it: You shall love your neighbor as yourself. On these two commandments depend all the Law and the Prophets" (Matt. 22:37b–40).

When we are waiting intensely, our eyes are focused on the future. We long for the home we don't have yet or a child to fill our arms or strength to return to our body. This focus on the future can keep us from seeing the people presently beside us. But God's command to love our neighbors won't wait until we have the neighbors we want. We must obey by loving those who are in our lives now.

Perhaps you are so ill that you are hospitalized. In the hospital, people cross your path all day long, even if you never get out of bed. They are your neighbors, and you should seek ways to love them. Maybe you are a single woman. Inviting others into your house for a meal or caring for another woman's children will allow you to practice hospitality and nurturing. Those gifts don't have to lie dormant just because you are unmarried. Or perhaps you feel like you need to wait for a "real home" before you can host a Bible study or community group. The people in your life need your hospitality now. The kingdom can't wait for you to buy your dream home.

Finally, if you are a believer, God has entrusted you with a message that the lost desperately need to hear. There is no more significant way to love your neighbors than to introduce them to the One who died for them.

Remembering the Goodness of God

In a time of deep darkness, I spent a lot of mornings meditating on Psalm 77. In this psalm, the writer feels abandoned. He lies awake all night, and the thought of God brings him pain rather than comfort because it appears that God has forgotten him.

Then he starts talking to himself. He remembers a time when he felt close to God and could see evidence of his favor. He asks himself a series of questions:

> Has his steadfast love forever ceased?
>> Are his promises at an end for all time?
> Has God forgotten to be gracious?
>> Has he in anger shut up his compassion? (Ps. 77:8–9)

Although you may be in a place where you feel forgotten by God, ask yourself, are you really the first person he has ever lost track of? Did his everlasting kindness that has endured for generations run out when it came to you? Asking myself such questions makes me feel ridiculous. Of course I've not been forgotten by God, no matter how far away he seems. The God who parted the Red Sea to make a pathway for his people can be trusted when it looks like I've hit a dead end.

Even if you don't think of yourself as a very theological person, it's important to ask yourself theological questions when your waiting leaves you doubting. Do you believe God is all-powerful? Do you believe that God is loving? Do you believe that God is good? If so, he has a purpose for your waiting, even if you cannot see it. Pastor and physician D. Martyn Lloyd-Jones contended that the best way to fight off spiritual depression was to talk to yourself rather than listen to yourself.[13] Like the psalmist, we must stop listening to our fears and start preaching to ourselves the goodness of God even when we can't see it clearly.

It is intensely annoying to be a passenger on a plane that has been ordered into a holding pattern, circling a destination rather than landing. It feels like being taken hostage by the sky. Most frustratingly, none of the passengers know how long the circling will last or whether it will cause them to miss their connecting flights.

As inconvenient as it is to be in a holding pattern, only a terrible pilot would stop circling simply to satisfy his passengers. Air traffic controllers command planes into holding patterns for a reason. Maybe there is a storm moving through, or maybe too many planes want to land at the same time. Imagine a pilot announcing over the loudspeaker, "Ladies and gentlemen, I've heard your frustration. I'm going to land in the next fifteen minutes whether I get clearance or not." While the passengers might cheer, their lives would be in grave danger.

No matter how aimless your waiting may seem, if you are God's child, he has a purpose for your holding pattern, and because he is good and loving, he will keep you in it until his purpose is accomplished.

Getting Swept Up in Others' Stories

There's nothing that takes my mind off my own struggles so well as a good story. I'm not talking about a romantic comedy or a best-selling page-turner. I'm talking about the stories of other Christians who have walked by faith through difficult days and demanding opposition.

Reading Christian biographies nourishes my faith and puts my life into perspective. I realize the challenges I'm facing pale in comparison to some of the trials others have withstood. Yet the source of their strength will be the source of mine, and God is no less willing to hear my prayers than he was to hear the prayers of the cloud of witnesses who've gone before me. He will provide for all my needs just as he provided for George Müller's. He will comfort me in loneliness just as he comforted Amy Carmichael. He can redeem my suffering just as he did for Olaudah Equiano, a former slave who became a British emancipator. Christian biographies make me long less for God's blessings and more for his glory.

You can also get swept up into stories by simply listening to other Christians. You are not the only one who is living a parable. Ask friends and acquaintances what they are waiting for. Ask church leaders what seasons of waiting they have walked through. Find out what sustained them. The school of waiting doesn't have to be a one-on-one tutorial between you and God alone. God has put other believers in your life to encourage you and to be encouraged by you, but that will only happen if you can put your own story out of your mind long enough to listen to someone else's.

Leaning Hard

We can allow our waiting to drive us from God or to drive us to him. Our burdens exist to make us lean all our weight upon the Lord. That truth is beautifully expressed in the following poem by Octavius Winslow:

> Child of my love, lean hard,
> And let me feel the pressure of thy care;
> I know thy burden, child, I shaped it;
> Poised it in mine own hand, made no proportion
> In its weight to thine unaided strength;
> For even as I laid it on, I said,
> "I shall be near, and while she leans on me,
> This burden shall be mine, not hers;
> So shall I keep my child within the circling arms of mine
> own love."
> Here lay it down, nor fear
> To impose it on a shoulder which upholds
> The government of worlds. Yet closer come;
> Thou art not near enough; I would embrace thy care
> So I might feel my child reposing on my breast.
> Thou lovest me? I knew it. Doubt not then
> But loving me, lean hard.[14]

You don't have to be strong or resourceful to wait well as you wait upon the Lord. You simply need to be willing to depend upon the Lord. He loves it when his children lean upon him.

8

When the Waiting Is Over

Ye fearful saints, fresh courage take;
The clouds ye so much dread
Are big with mercy and shall break
In blessings on your head.

William Cowper, "God Moves in a Mysterious Way"

I waited with one of my close friends and prayer partners through a long season of infertility. I grieved with her when a pregnancy ended in miscarriage. A couple of months after her miscarriage, we were praying on the phone, and I prayed again for a baby for her and her husband. After I finished my prayer, she whispered, "So I'm not supposed to tell yet, but . . . I'm pregnant."

It was so sweet to rejoice together over this new life in her womb, but just one day later, I received a tearful phone call. "I'm bleeding," she said. She hadn't been to the doctor yet, but all signs indicated that she had lost the baby. The next day during her doctor's appointment, I prayed for comfort for her in her grief. Imagine my surprise when I received a text message with the words, "BOTH babies are FINE." She was not only still pregnant, she was carrying twins! The fruits of her prayers and waiting now run around in the form of two identical little boys that delight and exhaust her.

Just at the point when it seemed like the waiting might never end, God had answered my friend's prayers even more abundantly than we expected. When that happens, the long wait takes on a beauty. In retrospect, we can hear the loveliness of the song, even though it was played in a minor key.

My Story Tells God's Story

I started writing this book after wrestling intensely with an unfulfilled desire for marriage. I knew that God was good. I knew that he would give me a husband if it was his best for me. What I struggled to understand was why he would allow me to miss out on the mystery of portraying Christ and the church.

When I realized that missing marriage didn't mean I had to miss out on telling God's story, my singleness became infused with purpose. My loneliness wasn't empty; it had a point. It was given to me by God to be a small picture of the longing that the church should feel as we yearn for our Bridegroom. Recognizing this didn't mean I had to view singleness or loneliness as good in themselves, but I could see how God could have a theological purpose for them even as I longed for marriage.

Although it felt uncomfortably vulnerable to talk about my unmet desires, I decided that if I wanted my story to tell God's story, I would have to share it. I did that by writing an article for The Gospel Coalition. It was called "Should I Be Content with My Singleness?" I said,

> If God ever gives me a husband, I will live out this picture of rejoicing in the long-awaited bridegroom. We'll have a wedding feast, which will foreshadow the marriage supper of the Lamb (Rev. 19:7–8). The purpose in my season of singleness will be obvious to everyone who shares in my rejoicing; it was to make the consummation all the sweeter.[15]

When I wrote those words, although I knew that it could happen, I didn't think that it would. I am very happy to have been wrong.

On May 23, 2014, the day after my article was published, I received an e-mail from a pastor in Manhattan. He didn't hit on me; he just thanked me for the article. A quick Google search revealed that he was single, originally from London, a Jewish Christian, and, not incidentally, quite handsome. I was intrigued. I wrote back, and we started corresponding. After a week of e-mailing, he suggested that we Skype. We talked for a couple of hours that first Skype, and at the end of our conversation, he asked in his pleasing English accent if he could fly down to Alabama and take me on a date.

On Thanksgiving Day, Bernard Nicholas Howard asked me to marry him. We were on a screened porch at my great-grandparents' farm. Somehow this tall, dashing British pastor had found his way to me in Alabama and ended my wait for a bridegroom. On May 23, exactly a year after he first wrote to me, I walked down the aisle to him. With no hesitation, I promised to love and cherish him as long as we both shall live. The wait—for him thirty-nine years, for me thirty-four—made finding each other even sweeter. Our friends and family feasted with us with pure and unrestrained joy.

The lessons I learned as a single woman and the promises I clung to haven't changed. Marriage was not the object of my article, and my singleness wasn't a problem to be solved. Singleness was God's will for me for one season of life, and now his will for me is marriage. The object of my life is the same: to glorify God and enjoy him forever. The parable, however, has changed. I am now living out the earthly picture of the heavenly reality of the church's oneness with Christ.

It felt like my situation turned on a dime. I woke up one morning with no marital prospects, and I went to bed wondering about a handsome British preacher. My life would never be the same.

Your Waiting Will End

Your life could change in a blink of an eye. I'm not talking about meeting the love of your life; I'm talking about meeting the One who loved you and gave himself up for you, who went away and promised to come again. Jesus Christ may return at any moment. No one knows the day or hour, so we must always watch and pray. When the wait gets long, you may start to think he's not coming. But one day, he will appear.

When a woman enters her ninth month of a pregnancy, everyone knows her baby must be born soon. In spite of this, I've watched friend after friend pass her due date and announce, "I'm starting to wonder if this baby is ever going to come." It's ironic that just at the point when she is heavy with child, a weary mother can start to lose hope that her baby will ever be born!

The same can be true of us as we wait for the coming of the kingdom. When days get dark, we disbelieve there will ever be a dawn. But the promises of God are sure, and delay is not denial.

Many of you reading this book will see an earthly end to your current season. If that happens, let it be a reminder and foretaste of the end to all your waiting. If God gives you a baby or a home, if he heals you or brings your prodigal to repentance, don't let it make you more at home in this world, but less. Let it increase your hunger for the day when all your desires will be satisfied.

Don't Be Caught Unawares

The text for our wedding sermon was the parable of the ten virgins from Matthew 25. The preacher, Simon Tomkins, did an excellent job making it relevant to the congregation.

He had us imagine that ten bridesmaids have been sent in two cars to meet a groom at the airport, but the groom's flight has been delayed. Neither of the bridesmaids' cars has a full tank of gas. The delay gives them plenty of time to fill up their cars before the groom's arrival, and five of the bridesmaids in one car use their waiting time to do just that. The other bridesmaids see no need to rush because they have a long wait ahead of them.

Perhaps the pilot of the groom's plane made up some of the lost time because, suddenly, the flight arrives. The groom is before them, and the wait is over. This is good news for the bridesmaids with a full tank of gas, and they take the groom directly to the wedding. The other five bridesmaids still have to fill up their tank. It takes them so long to find a station that they run out of gas. To their great distress, they miss the wedding completely. Rev. Tomkins concluded, "The punchline comes in verse 13: 'Watch therefore, for you know neither the day nor the hour.' Jesus is saying, it's foolish not to get ready for something we know is going to happen just because we don't know when it's going to happen."

It is possible to wait for something without being ready for it. You might be waiting for Jesus, but are you ready for his return?

We need to order our earthly lives in such a way that Christ's second coming fulfills and completes all that we are working for rather than interrupts it.

Foretastes of the Kingdom

Every time a once-barren woman holds her child in her arms, she tastes the joy that waits for us in the kingdom of God. When a mother opens the door to see her long-estranged son, when she holds him safely in her arms, she tastes the reconciliation that is to come when God gathers his children. When a single mother who has lived in shelter after shelter moves into her own home and hangs a swing for her child from a tree in their own back-yard, she tastes the peace that will be hers in her heavenly home. When a scan comes back clean and a doctor tells a patient she is cancer free, when she can once again take part in all of life's pleasures that chemo had left her too weak to enjoy, she tastes the health that will be hers when she is given a resurrected body. And when a new bride lies in her husband's arms after years of going to sleep alone, she tastes the covenant love that will be ours in Christ for all eternity.

Both the waiting and the end of the waiting tell God's story. If you hope in God though your dream is unfulfilled, you walk by faith and not by sight. If you praise God when your dream comes true and you look beyond that dream to an even better fulfillment, you show yourself to be a citizen of heaven.

There's a tension here, and it can be very tempting to resolve that tension in a way that is unbiblical. It's wrong to make an idol of your dreams and refuse to be content unless they are fulfilled. But it is also wrong to stop praying for the fulfillment of your desires if they are God honoring. Sometimes it's easier not to want and therefore stand no risk of disappointment, but

God calls us out of our safety and tells us to entrust our hearts to his keeping.

Theologian D. A. Carson says that we must get used to living in tension because it won't fully be resolved until the last day:

> We await the return of Jesus Christ, the arrival of the new heaven and the new earth, the dawning of the resurrection, the glory of perfection, the beauty of holiness. Until that day, we are a people in tension. On the one hand, we belong to the broader culture in which we find ourselves; on the other, we belong to the culture of the consummated kingdom of God, which has dawned among us. Our true city is the new Jerusalem, even while we still belong to Paris or Budapest or New York. And while we await the consummation, we gratefully and joyfully confess that the God of all is our God, and that we have been called to give him glory, acknowledge his reign, and bear witness to his salvation.[16]

The tension you feel as you try to simultaneously hope in heaven while living wholeheartedly in this life isn't necessarily an indicator of sinful discontentment. It may simply be evidence that you are a citizen of heaven living on earth.

In the midst of waiting, it can be very hard to see the purpose of it. Sometimes we can see purpose once we come out on the other side of our wait. Your long wait for a child may seem purposeful once you hold in your arms the son or daughter God had appointed for you, a child who hadn't even been born when you started a lengthy adoption process. While you were waiting for a home, God may have moved you from city to city because he had people in those places who would change your life.

I don't know why God waited until I was thirty-four to bring me a husband. He could have done it much sooner. When I was twenty, I spent a semester abroad in Oxford, England. My future husband was living and working in that very city; in fact, we were both active in the same evangelical church. Week after week, I went to church on Sunday morning and Sunday night, wishing that one of the godly British men would look my way. My bridegroom was in the room, but I didn't meet him.

In hindsight, both Bernard and I believe that if we had met when I was twenty, we probably wouldn't have married each other. We both had a great deal of growing to do to be a good fit as a couple. Please don't mistake my meaning: I don't believe God waits for a certain level of spiritual maturity before he will bring someone a spouse; that's a lie that Christians sometimes perpetuate. Rather, I believe God knew all along that Bernard was the man he had prepared for me, but he waited to bring him into my life at a time when I was primed to recognize that.

If you glimpse purpose on the other side of your waiting, that's a foretaste of the understanding that will be ours when all our waiting is finished. Romans 8:28 is one of the most precious promises in God's Word; don't let its familiarity numb you to the boldness of the claim:

> And we know that for those who love God all things work together for good, for those who are called according to his purpose.

God has a purpose, it is good for you, and he is working it out through your waiting. At the moment, waiting may feel good for you in the way that medicine is good for a child. He may only swallow it because his parent gives him no choice. But one day, you will see fully and affirm the goodness of the purpose with no hesitation: "For now we see in a mirror dimly, but then face to face. Now I know in part; then I shall know fully, even as I have been fully known" (1 Cor. 13:12). If your earthly waiting ends and you glimpse God's ways, that is only a dim reflection of the glorious purposes that will one day be revealed.

Waiting Well When Your Waiting Is Over

When your waiting ends, your waiting has not ended. Until we are safely home in the presence of Christ, we live in a fallen world in earthly tents. If you finally have the thing you've been waiting for, don't mistake the joy it brings for ultimate joy. We have an enemy, and he likes to take God's blessings and turn them into idols.

The people of Israel waited for generations for God to deliver them from slavery in Egypt. One day that waiting ended when God raised up Moses, and Pharaoh finally let the people go. Their rich Egyptian neighbors sent them away laden with silver and gold. One day they had been slaves, and the next they were liberated and wealthy.

The gold of Egypt should have been used to build God a temple in the Promised Land. Instead, the people used it to make an idol, a golden calf (Exodus 32). They took God's blessings, and instead of offering them back to him, they worshiped them.

Don't let Satan turn God's blessings into idols. Don't worship the created thing instead of the Creator. Hold every earthly blessing out to God with open hands. If you desire to keep your heart from idols, God will help you avoid the snares and temptations of the Evil One, "For the eyes of the LORD range throughout the earth to strengthen those whose hearts are fully committed to him" (2 Chron. 16:9a NIV).

Conclusion

What Are We Waiting For?

On Jordan's stormy banks I stand,
And cast a wishful eye
To Canaan's fair and happy land,
Where my possessions lie.
I am bound for the promised land,
I am bound for the promised land;
Oh who will come and go with me?
I am bound for the promised land.

Samuel Stennett, "On Jordan's Stormy Banks I Stand"

My husband is Jewish. At our wedding, we observed two Jewish traditions. First, we said our marriage vows under a chuppah. The chuppah is a small tent, and it symbolizes the start of a new household. It also reminds us that Abraham and Sarah, the father and mother of Israel, lived out their days in a tent. They were sojourners until the day they died, "looking forward to the city that has foundations, whose designer and builder is God" (Heb. 11:10).

The second Jewish tradition in our wedding was the breaking of a glass. After the marriage is pronounced, the groom stomps upon a wine glass (wrapped in a cloth), producing a decisive and satisfying shattering sound. This curious custom symbolizes the destruction of the temple in Jerusalem in AD 70. It reminds the congregation that even at the happiest moment of one's life, joy is tempered with sorrow because God's temple has been destroyed. All is not right with the world.

So at the happiest of moments for Jewish newlyweds, they remember that they are not home yet. The new home that they make together will be a temporary dwelling place. They must look forward to a future promised restoration. As new covenant believers, we know that that full restoration will come only when Jesus Christ returns and brings with him the New Jerusalem.

At the moment when I became a wife, the shattered glass reminded me that "happily ever after" will not begin until we are welcomed into that holy city. My singleness ended with my marriage, but I'm a sinful woman married to a sinful man in a fallen world. There is more pain and waiting ahead. But beyond that, we have this beautiful hope that we will be claimed by our heavenly Bridegroom who makes all things new: "He will wipe away every tear from their eyes, and death shall be no more, neither shall there be mourning, nor crying, nor pain anymore, for the former things have passed away" (Rev. 21:4). Even if your season of waiting ends, your life of waiting will continue, if you are waiting for that eternal home.

Wait for the Sake of the World

What are we waiting for? Beyond the blessings we wait for, what purpose is there in our waiting? I've made the case that your story can tell God's story as you put your hope in eternal blessings rather than temporal satisfaction. If you wait with a heart fixed on God's promises, you will bring him great glory.

If you are willing to let your story tell God's story, non-Christians will notice. The world doesn't understand waiting. It tells the single woman she shouldn't wait for marriage for sexual fulfillment. It tells the barren woman that she just hasn't found the right doctor yet. It tells the woman waiting for a home that if she could get a better job and buy her dream house, her homesickness would go away. It says to the woman waiting for healing that she needs to make the most of the time she has left because that's all there is. It tells the woman waiting for a prodigal child that she must not have read the right parenting books and the woman waiting for a prodigal spouse that she married the wrong person.

When we reject these worldly messages and choose to wait in faith, we stand out. We may even look a little odd. People who refuse to live for themselves and pour their lives out on behalf of others *are* odd. They are culturally abnormal because the kingdom of heaven operates by a different set of norms. If you hope in something that this world doesn't offer, people are going to want to know the reason, and the Bible commands us to be prepared to give one (1 Pet. 3:15).

The world understands how we can trust God when everything in our lives is going well. What it doesn't understand is why we still cling to God when he takes everything away. When God allowed Job's life to fall apart, Job's response was, "Though he slay me, I will hope in him" (Job 13:15a). Job's hope was not unfounded. When your neighbors want to know how you keep going through cancer treatment, tell them about the new body you've been promised at the end of God's story. If they want to know how you can hold your head up after being abandoned by your husband, tell them about your faithful God who pursues prodigals such as you and me. Let your story tell God's story.

While I was writing this book, a good friend was diagnosed with what would prove to be a fatal illness. She endured days of dreadful physical suffering. Those of us who loved her longed for her to be out of her misery. But I had to check my desire for her relief because my friend was an unbeliever. If she did not repent of her sins and trust Christ for her salvation, death would not bring an end to her suffering.

Every day that Christ tarries is a day for those who still have life and breath to repent. When it seems unkind for God to make us wait so many years for Christ's return, we must remember the words of Peter: "The Lord is not slow to fulfill his promise as some count slowness, but is patient toward you, not wishing that any should perish, but that all should reach repentance" (2 Pet. 3:9).

For those of us who are believers, everything that we are waiting for will ultimately be satisfied in the life to come. The opposite is true for the unbeliever. The lost soul who suffers pain, loneliness, and broken relationships experiences a very small taste of the misery that awaits her in eternity. As you wait for your coming Bridegroom, let the suffering of this life compel you to do everything in your power to save others from the suffering that never ends.

Wait for the Sake of the Church

Friends wait with each other. When your loved one is undergoing life-threatening surgery, your friends are going to be in the waiting room holding your hand. If your sister is giving birth, you want to be close by. There's no actual benefit to being in the hospital waiting room during a birth or an operation, but in times of intense waiting, we want to be close to the people we love.

When we wait in community, we help each other keep the promises of God in view. Just as you need your friend in the hospital waiting room to hold your hand, we need to be in each other's lives to remind one another where we are heading. The writer of Hebrews urges, "And let us consider how to stir up one another to love and good works, not neglecting to meet together, as is the habit of some, but encouraging one another, and all the more as you see the Day drawing near" (Heb. 10:24–25).

We are waiting for the Day. The Day is drawing near. Members of the body of Christ are meant to help each other remember how fleeting this time will be. In hindsight, when our waiting is over, it won't feel like it lasted very long. It's a bit like the way time moves for parents. Parenting has cleverly been called "the longest shortest time." Mothers of small children are told by older women, "they are going to grow up before you know it," although sometimes the hours (especially those between naptime and dinnertime) can crawl by. But one day, those hours will be over and the days will have passed in a flash. Your children will be grown. The other mothers who told you, "they will eventually sleep through the night" and "they aren't going to wet the bed forever" will have been proved right.

Your waiting may feel long right now. But one day, you will see that it was "the longest shortest time." Just as young mothers need older mothers to help them stay the course, we need to help each other trust God that our waiting won't last forever. We need to tell each other, "You won't always ache like this."

The apostle Paul wasn't shy about telling other believers to imitate him (Phil. 3:17; 2 Thess. 3:7). If you are waiting well, your perseverance will give you credibility to urge others to walk by faith in their waiting. While "I know how you feel" may ring hollow when it comes from the wrong person, those words in the mouth of someone who has also endured a long season of waiting are incredibly powerful.

If you are living through your own season of waiting, you know how strong the temptation can be for a single woman when she is romantically pursued by an unbeliever. You can imagine the pull of bitterness felt by the woman with a barren womb. You know the weariness of the woman who has never had a home, the doubts of a woman who may never be well again, and the consuming distraction of someone who loves a prodigal. Even if you aren't waiting for the same thing, you can in some sense say, "I know how you feel." Whenever you find yourself speaking those words, let it be a small reminder that your waiting has not been in vain.

Embrace the Giver

Although this book is at an end, my waiting is not. True, I am no longer waiting for a bridegroom, but rarely does one waiting season end without another beginning. I don't know if God will give us children, but I am praying that he will. If he does, our small apartment will seem even smaller. We will be waiting for a home in a city where even a one-bedroom apartment rents for a staggering amount of money. My husband and I have moved far from our families with the dream of planting a church here, but we must wait to see if God fulfills that dream. Until Christ returns, I will always be waiting on something.

I still struggle with wanting God's gifts more than I want him. But I'm grateful that God continues to withhold some of his gifts in order to satisfy me with himself. The presence of God in the darkness of our trials is a small foretaste of the presence of God that we will know in the eternal light of his glory. It is in the absence of God's gifts that I learn the Giver himself is the greatest gift of all.

I said in the first chapter that God wasn't looking for us to learn our lesson so that we could move on from waiting, and that is true. But one day, we will graduate from the school of waiting. We won't have graduated on our own merits. But if Jesus is your hope, all your dreams will be fulfilled on that day. There won't be any doubt in your mind about what you have waited for. You were waiting for Jesus.

Acknowledgments

To each of the women who let me tell her story in this book, thank you. Your stories have helped me better understand and believe God's story.

I'm grateful for everyone at Crossway that helped make this book possible. Special thanks to Justin Taylor, Laura Talcott, Amy Kruis, Angie Cheatham, and Lane and Ebeth Dennis.

My coworkers at Beeson Divinity School and now at The Gospel Coalition have sharpened my thinking and shaped my story. It's wonderful to work with people I would choose to have as friends.

Collin Hansen and Gloria Furman patiently helped me work through the concept, proposal, and manuscript for this book, and Kathleen Nielson read an early copy and made thoughtful suggestions.

I am so thankful for friends who have walked with me over the years in prayer groups and Bible studies. You have been excellent companions on the wait.

Thank you to my parents, siblings, and extended family members who have always read everything I've written through the extremely biased filter of their love for me.

I am grateful to my husband, Bernard, for redirecting my story in a very welcome way. Thank you for urging me to write this book when I wanted to turn back. Thank you for the many hours you spent helping me to improve it. Thank you for daily directing my gaze to our heavenly Bridegroom.

Notes

1. The various examples of women in different seasons of waiting that I share throughout this book are all friends of mine, though I have changed their names.
2. Andrew Murray, *Waiting on God* (Radford, VA: Wilder, 2008), 64.
3. Sally Lloyd-Jones, *The Jesus Storybook Bible* (Grand Rapids, MI: Zondervan, 2007), 17.
4. Helmut Thielicke, "The Parable of the Wise and Foolish Maidens," *The Waiting Father: Sermons on the Parables of Jesus*, trans. John W. Doberstein (New York: Harper & Brothers, 1959), 176.
5. For a thorough explanation of the Bible's teaching on same-sex relations, see Kevin DeYoung, *What Does the Bible Really Teach about Homosexuality?* (Wheaton, IL: Crossway, 2015).
6. Elisabeth Elliot, *Passion and Purity* (Grand Rapids, MI: Revell, 2002), 66–67.
7. S. Pearce Carey, MA, *William Carey, D. D.: Fellow of Linnaean Society* (London: Hodder & Stoughton, 1923), 41.
8. G. K. Chesterton, "The House of Christmas" in *Poems* by Gilbert Keith Chesterton (New York: Dodd, Mead, and Company, 1922), 63–64.
9. C. S. Lewis, *Mere Christianity* (New York: Harper Collins, 1952), 135.
10. Augustine, *Confessions*, trans. Henry Chadwick (Oxford: Oxford University Press, 1991), 3.
11. C. S. Lewis, letter to Mary Willis Shelburne, in *The Collected Letters of C. S. Lewis*, 3 vols. (New York: Harper Collins, 2007), 3:776.
12. Vaneetha Rendall, "When God Does the Miracle We Didn't Ask For," February 8, 2014, http://www.desiringgod.org/articles /when-god-does-the-miracle-we-didn-t-ask-for.
13. D. Martyn Lloyd-Jones, *Spiritual Depression: Its Causes and Cures* (Grand Rapids, MI: Eerdmans, 1995), 20.

14. Octavius Winslow, *The Ministry of Home* (London: William Hunt & Co., 1867), 355.
15. Betsy Childs, "Should I Be Content with My Singleness?" May 22, 2014, http://www.thegospelcoalition.org/article /should-i-be-content-with-my-singleness.
16. D. A. Carson, *Christ and Culture Revisited* (Grand Rapids, MI: Eerdmans, 2012), 64.

General Index

Scripture Index

THE GOSPEL COALITION

The Gospel Coalition is a fellowship of evangelical churches deeply committed to renewing our faith in the gospel of Christ and to reforming our ministry practices to conform fully to the Scriptures. We have committed ourselves to invigorating churches with new hope and compelling joy based on the promises received by grace alone through faith alone in Christ alone.

We desire to champion the gospel with clarity, compassion, courage, and joy—gladly linking hearts with fellow believers across denominational, ethnic, and class lines. We yearn to work with all who, in addition to embracing our confession and theological vision for ministry, seek the lordship of Christ over the whole of life with unabashed hope in the power of the Holy Spirit to transform individuals, communities, and cultures.

Through its women's initiatives, The Gospel Coalition aims to support the growth of women in faithfully studying and sharing the Scriptures; in actively loving and serving the church; and in spreading the gospel of Jesus Christ in all their callings.

Join the cause and visit TGC.org for fresh resources that will equip you to love God with all your heart, soul, mind, and strength, and to love your neighbor as yourself.

Also Available from the Gospel Coalition

To see the full list of books published in partnership
with the Gospel Coalition, visit crossway.org/TGC.